The Wanderlust World Travel Quiz Book

Thousands of questions for everyone from the
armchair traveller to the experienced globetrotter

WELBECK

CONTENTS

INTRODUCTION

When the coronavirus pandemic put a stop to world travel in 2020, one thing didn't halt – *Wanderlust* magazine readers' love for a travel quiz.

In fact, the quizzes shared each week on the Wanderlust website only grew in popularity as March turned into summer and beyond – perhaps because they allowed us all to travel vicariously while the world was grounded.

So the natural next step was to compile this travel quiz book. Of course, no matter how much and how far you've travelled, no one has seen and done everything. It has therefore been written with different interests in mind, so you can choose your favourite topics.

There are several themes – general quizzes with a geography bent, natural wonders, manmade marvels, colourful wildlife-themed quizzes, photo-based posers, trivia tests focused on the world's greatest explorers and journeys, plus a random chapter of quizzes that are 'just for fun' – to suit every style of traveller.

Some chapters are easier than others, and I've assumed a certain level of interest and knowledge. I've aimed to make every quiz fun and challenging – and will hopefully inspire a future trip or two.

On a personal note, I am thrilled to have written this book. All those years of obsessing over how to visit as many countries as possible on a single trip have finally paid off. I really hope you enjoy it.

Inevitably, mistakes may have slipped in, or things may have changed, so if you do spot anything, please do contact Wanderlust so they can be amended in future editions. Now, get quizzing...

Elizabeth Atkin, September 2020

AROUND THE GLOBE

Love Canada? Can't get enough of Australia?
Perhaps your chosen travel destination involves
multiple countries in Central Asia or South
America? Whatever your travel preference,
there's a quiz here for you.

Each quiz is organised by region – 21 regions
to be exact. We've split up Europe, Africa, Asia,
the Americas and beyond, so you can test your
specific travel knowledge.

Time to set off around the globe and see
how much you really know! Good luck…

NORTHERN EUROPE

1. By total area, which Baltic country is biggest: Estonia, Latvia or Lithuania?

2. By population, which Nordic capital is bigger: Stockholm or Helsinki?

3. Which Nordic country's flag is white with a blue cross?

4. The UNESCO-inscribed Ilulissat Icefjord is part of which northern country?

5. In which Scandinavian country would you most likely tuck into *rakfisk*, sometimes called the world's smelliest fish dish?

6. Lake Saimaa is the largest lake in which country?

7. What is the name of the northernmost point in mainland Europe? Here's a clue: it begins with 'Cape'

8. Nordic noir TV series *The Bridge* is set in Sweden and Denmark. But what is the name of the bridge?

9. Can you name the four countries Latvia shares a border with?

10. Which of the five Nordic countries and three Baltic countries has the most UNESCO sites?

11. What is the world's largest land carnivore, found in Norway's Arctic Svalbard archipelago?

12. From which country does the concept of *hygge* (cosy living) originate?

13. Which northern European country has a yellow, green and red-striped flag?

14. What is the name of Copenhagen's autonomous (and controversial) commune?

15. Roughly how many islands make up the Stockholm archipelago?

16. In which century was Riga's House of the Blackheads built?

17. Which bird that breeds in Iceland undertakes the world's longest migration, an annual return flight to Antarctica?

18. Between which northern countries' coasts does the Gulf of Bothnia lie?

19. Gauja is the largest and oldest national park of which country?

20. Which northern country is home to one of the world's only phallological museums?

21. In which country would you find the picturesque Flåm Railway?

22. Is Iceland's travel hotspot Vatnajökull A) a volcano, B) a hot spring, or C) an ice cap?

23. Which northern sea is the world's largest expanse of brackish water?

24. Svalbard, Spitsbergen and Longyearbyen are alluring destinations in Arctic Norway. But which is a town, which is an island, and which is an archipelago?

EASTERN EUROPE

1. Which is the largest by area: Ukraine, Romania or Belarus?

2. Which is the smallest by area: Moldova, Armenia or Georgia?

3. What title has the Romanian city of Timisoara been awarded for 2021?

4. Moldova's Old Orhei monastery complex dates back to which century?

5. How much of Belarus is covered in forest: 16%, 27% or 38%?

6. Which Eastern European country's flag has a horizontal blue stripe above a yellow stripe?

7. Georgians have a particular fondness for which nut?

8. Which has the larger population: Ukraine or Belarus?

9. The Caucasus mountain range extends over Russia and which three countries?

10. What's the main official language of Moldova?

11. Which Eastern European country has the world's heaviest building, featuring over 3,500 tons of crystal glass?

12. The autonomous majority-Armenian region of Nagorno-Karabakh (Artsakh) is claimed by which other country?

13. The striking wavy structure called the Flame Towers is in which capital city?

14. In which city and country would you find the unusually-arched Bridge of Peace over the Kura River?

15. Rynok Square and the Lychakiv Cemetery can be found in which Ukrainian city?

16. Which Eastern European country is home to the world's oldest winery?

17. In which century was Azerbaijan's famous and historic Maiden Tower built?

18. The exclusion zone around the site of the Chernobyl nuclear disaster is now a popular tourism destination. Which other European country has its own Chernobyl Exclusion Zone?

19. In which Eastern European capital would you find the Cascade Complex stair/waterfall?

20. In which two countries would you eat the maize porridge mamaliga?

21. In which country does the word *dyakuyu* mean 'thank you'?

22. In which Eastern European capital would you find the artificial Island of Tears?

23. Which two Romanian cities have their own Hollywood-style signs high in the hills?

24. Svaneti and Tusheti are regions known for mountain scenery, fortified tower houses and traditional culture in which country?

25. Apricot is the national fruit of which Eastern European country?

26. Can you name the highest peak in Georgia, at 5,193m tall?

CENTRAL EUROPE

1. Which country is bigger by area: Germany or Poland?

2. Which is the smallest Central European country by area?

3. Which Viennese building, noted for its irregular pink, blue, yellow and white patchwork, was named for the renowned local artist who designed it?

4. Where is the oldest working astronomical clock in the world?

5. The flag of which country comprises horizontal black, red and yellow stripes?

6. With which Central European country are *pierogi* (filled dumplings) most associated?

7. In which country is Balaton, the largest lake in Central Europe?

8. The fascinating and UNESCO-listed Wieliczka Salt Mine can be found in which country?

9. How high does Bled Castle sit above Lake Bled in Slovenia: 30m, 80m or 130m?

10. The Central European brandy known in Slovakia as *slivovica* is made with which fruit?

11. Between which two cities in Germany does the Romantic Road run?

12. In which Central European country could you ride the Glacier Express Railway?

13. In which Central European country is the city of eský Krumlov?

14. Neptune Fountain and Oliwa Cathedral are two gems in which Polish city?

15. Which of these animals can be found in the High Tatras, Slovakia – brown bears, wolves, lynx?

16. The Istria peninsula is shared by Slovenia and which two Southern European countries?

17. What is the currency of Poland?

18. In which Austrian city can you visit the birthplace of Wolfgang Amadeus Mozart?

19. Budapest has two parts, separated by the Danube: Buda and Pest. Which side is bigger (and busier)?

20. In which year did the Berlin Wall fall – 1988, 1989 or 1990?

21. Liechtenstein is a small country. To the nearest km, how long is it: 25km, 50km or 75km?

22. A visit to Hungary is not complete without at least a taste of beef goulash. Can you name this famous dish's key spice?

23. Which famously pointed mountain looms above Zermatt in the Swiss Alps?

24. In which Central European city and country can you walk through Michael's Gate?

25. Which Central European city is nicknamed 'the City of 100 Spires'?

26. Fürstensteig is the most famous mountain hike in which Central European country?

SOUTHERN EUROPE

1. Which Southern European country is largest by area: Italy, Portugal or Spain?

2. Which Southern European country is smallest by area: Andorra, Vatican City or San Marino?

3. What's the official name of Greece?

4. How many national parks does Croatia have – 3, 6 or 8?

5. In which city and (small) country would you find the Església de Sant Esteve church?

6. Gibraltar is an overseas territory of which country?

7. On which Italian island is the active volcano Mount Etna?

8. Which species of bear might you come across in Tara National Park, Serbia?

9. In which Southern European capital would you find the old bazaar of Baščaršija?

10. In which Southern European country would you find The Blue Eye, a natural spring with an unknown depth?

11. Fira, Pyrgos and Perissa are all villages on which Greek island?

12. Which country is famous for its small size, early use of stamps and for having Abraham Lincoln as an honorary citizen?

13. Which Southern European capital is also one of the world's most popular girl's names?

14. The village of Blagaj, home to a famous Dervish monastery, is in which country?

15. In which capital would you find the Pyramid, an unusual 1980s structure harking back to the era of communism?

16. Zamora, Spain, and Porto, Portugal, sit on which river?

17. The historic city of Ohrid, a UNESCO World Heritage Site, is in which country?

18. The Rugova Mountains are found in which country?

19. Kotor, Montenegro gets its name from an Old Greek word describing the weather or temperature. What does it mean?

20. Liguria, Italy is the birthplace of which green sauce?

21. In which country is Zlatni Rat Beach (or Golden Horn), known for its vivid blue water and shifting sand?

22. Oplenac Mausoleum, burial place of the Karadordevic royal house known for its opulent mosaic, is in the town of Topola – in which country?

23. Évora, Sines and Beja are cities in which rural region of Portugal?

24. Which ancient fortified town is often called 'the Silent City of Malta'?

25. In which Southern European country would you find Međugorje's Risen Christ Statue?

26. The entertaining La Tomatina festival usually takes place in which Spanish town and region?

WESTERN EUROPE

1. Which is bigger by area: France, Belgium or Ireland?

2. Which Western Europe countries are known as the three Low Countries?

3. Where is Flemish most often spoken in Western Europe?

4. Are Le Mont Saint Michel in France and Saint Michael's Mount in the UK both tidal islands?

5. For which sweet delicacy is the Belgian artisan Maison Pierre Marcolini famed?

6. What is Northern Ireland's highest peak and its county?

7. The Chiltern Hills, Cotswolds and Kent Downs all share which English countryside designation?

8. If you were munching on the dish *cuisses de grenouille* in a French restaurant, what would you be eating?

9. In which year did Galway, Ireland hold the title of European Capital of Cuture?

10. In which Western European city and country would you find the 11th-century Sint-Janshospitaal?

11. Is the wingspan of England's Angel of the North statue: 23m, 34m or 54m?

12. How many windmills are there in the Netherlands' UNESCO-listed Kinderdijk site?

13. Which French region is known for its lavender fields?

14. What are *bitterballen*, and in which Western European country would you be most likely to eat them?

15. Does the UK have a bigger population than France?

16. The glorious Brecon Beacons National Park is in which region of Wales: north or south?

17. What is Luxembourg's full, official name?

18. Which Scottish city is known as the 'Granite City'?

19. In which century was Amsterdam's canal ring completed?

20. Which 14km-long Irish cliffs featured in the films *The Princess Bride* (1987) and *Harry Potter and the Half-Blood Prince* (2009)?

21. In which architectural style was the 19th-century Arc de Triomphe in Paris built?

22. Adolphe Bridge is part of which old and architecturally gorgeous Western European UNESCO site?

23. Texel National Park in the Netherlands is best known for what natural feature?

24. An easy one for peak-baggers. Can you name Scotland's highest peak?

25. The Wild Atlantic Way is one of Western Europe's great road trips. In which country can you drive it?

26. Roughly how much of the Netherlands lies below sea level: one-third or two-thirds?

RUSSIA

1. Russia encompasses what proportion of the Earth's landmass: 5%, 10% or 20%?

2. In Russia, what is an *oblast*?

3. A village in Russia is the world's coldest inhabited place, according to Guinness World Records. Can you name the village and guess its lowest temperature?

4. How long is the Volga River: 3,530km or 5,350km?

5. The most famous square in Russia's capital, Moscow, is named after which colour?

6. From 1914 to 1924, Saint Petersburg had a different name. Do you know what it was?

7. In which Russian city is the Bronze Horseman statue?

8. Which currency would you use on a trip to Russia?

9. The Moscow Kremlin overlooks which red, green and blue cathedral?

10. Which Siberian city is known for its state ballet, which is housed in a theatre nicknamed the Siberian Coliseum?

11. In which Russian city would you find the Amber Museum?

12. The national flower of Russia is considered to be very calming and healing. Do you know what it is?

13. The huge national park gazetted in 2012, spanning nearly 2800 sq km near Vladivostock, is named for the critically endangered local subspecies of which creature?

14. Which museum holds an annual celebration event for its cats?

15. *Pelmeni* is the Russian version of which popular food?

16. In which mountain range will you find Mount Elbrus, Russia's highest mountain?

17. In which city in Russia would you find the Winter Palace?

18. The beautiful walk from Listvyanka to Bolshie Hoty winds through forests and along the shore of which icy Russian lake?

19. Which Russian city on the Volga is known for its UNESCO-listed Kremlin, built from the 16th century for Ivan the Terrible?

20. Who founded Saint Petersburg's famous Hermitage Museum in 1764?

21. Ferries from Vladivostok sail to which Japanese port?

22. Russia's flag features three horizontal red, white and blue stripes. In which order are the colours arranged, from top to bottom?

23. Which 1200km-long peninsula in the Russian Far East is known for its volcanoes and wildlife, including brown bears and salmon?

24. The world's largest wild cat is endangered but still found in Russia. What is it called?

25. Which mountain range in Russia is often called 'the Gateway to Asia'?

CENTRAL ASIA

1. The Central Asian 'stan nations are Kazakhstan, Kyrgyzstan, Tajikistan, Uzbekistan and Turkmenistan. Which is the biggest by area?

2. Which is the smallest Central Asian 'stan by area?

3. What is the meaning of the word 'stan'?

4. Which mountainous 'stan was voted the Top Emerging Destination in the Wanderlust Reader Travel Awards 2020?

5. In which Central Asian country would you find Karl Marx Peak?

6. Turkmenistan is home to the 'Gate of Hell', a fiery gas crater called Darvaza. When is it believed to have started burning: 1961, 1971 or 1981?

7. In which Central Asian country would you find the otherworldly Lake Kaindy?

8. In which Uzbek city would you find the jaw-dropping Registan?

9. If you were to play *kes kumay* in Kyrgyzstan, which game would you be playing?

10. The start and end of the Pamir Highway is sometimes disputed, but in which country is most of its length?

11. The eye-catching, Art Deco Ismoili Somoni Monument can be found in which Central Asian city?

12. In which Central Asian city could you stroll through the domed Chorsu Market?

13. Kalan Mosque and Bolo Hauz Mosque are found in which Uzbek city?

14. What is the Central Asian dish of *laghman*, which is popular in Kazakhstan, Kyrgyzstan and Uzbekistan?

15. In which two countries is traditional hunting with eagles still practised?

16. On which protected Tajik lake could you find a plethora of birdlife including the stunning red-mantled rosefinch and saker falcon?

17. The beautiful, 80km-long Charyn Canyon can be found in which Central Asian country?

18. Are all five of the Central Asia 'stans former Soviet republics?

19. What transit system in Uzbekistan is famous for its ornate and beautiful stations?

20. The Tian Shan wapiti is a species of which animal?

21. *Tipin enemei* is another of Kyrgyzstan's traditional horseriding sports. In this one, what are you doing while on the horse?

22. Berkut is the Central Asian name for which bird?

23. Zenkov Cathedral, Kok Tobe and the Park of 28 Panfilov Guardsmen can be found in which Central Asian city?

24. In which country can you visit the ruins of the ancient city of Merv, one of the most important stops on the Silk Road?

MIDDLE EAST

1. Which Middle Eastern country is largest by area: Iran, Turkey or Egypt?

2. The tallest structure in Egypt is known colloquially as Nasser's Pineapple. But what is its correct name?

3. In which Middle Eastern country could you hike the mountain Jebel Shams?

4. The atmospheric Akdamar Island belongs to which Middle Eastern country?

5. What is said to have happened to Jesus Christ on the site of Jerusalem's Church of the Holy Sepulchre?

6. *Maqluba* is a Middle Eastern dish. What is unusual about how it's served?

7. Which city in Iran is famous for the Unesco-listed Naqsh-e Jahan square?

8. How many metres deep in Saudi Arabia's Al-Waba Crater: 100m, 250m or 500m?

9. In which Middle Eastern country would you find the crescent-shaped Banana Island?

10. Baalbek in Lebanon was thought to be built in which year: 9,000BC, 4,000BC or 200AD?

11. Which archaeological wonder in Jordan is known as the 'Rose Red City'?

12. What is the capital city of Bahrain?

13. Which magnificent desert ecosystem in Jordan, dubbed the 'Valley of the Moon', is home to Bedouin camps in which you can spend the night?

14. The dive sites at Yamanieh Coral Reef are near which Middle Eastern city?

15. The Pearl-Qatar is a luxury real-estate island in which Qatari city?

16. Karnak and Valley of the Queens can be explored near which Egyptian city?

17. What is Egypt's time zone?

18. In which country can you admire Baatara Gorge Waterfall?

19. Mocha coffee is named after a city in which country?

20. Hagia Sophia and the Grand Bazaar are in which Turkish city?

21. How many domes adorn the iconic Sheikh Zayed Grand Mosque in Abu Dhabi: 22, 52 or 82?

22. What's the full name of the coastal city of Tel Aviv, Israel?

23. *Molokhia*, a soup popular in the Middle East, is made with leaves from which plant?

24. The Jordan, Sinai, Lebanon Mountain and Abraham are all long-distance what?

25. Following World War II, which capital became known as 'The Paris of the East'?

26. Which Middle Eastern country has the longest Red Sea coastline?

AFRICA & INDIAN OCEAN

1. Which Northern African country is bigger by area: Morocco or Tunisia?

2. Roughly, how many animal species live in Kenya: 11,000, 19,000 or 25,000?

3. What's the name of the town on the Zambian side of Victoria Falls?

4. The Moorish Blue Gate and Chouara Tannery can be found in which Moroccan city?

5. Chott el Jerid, a Tunisian salt lake, stars as a location in which sci-fi movie franchise?

6. The desert sparrow is commonly found in which North African desert?

7. Which Eastern African country is bigger by area: Mozambique, Ethiopia or Tanzania?

8. What's the name of the long geographical feature tracing a faultline nearly the length of the continent?

9. Can you name the largest of the Comoros Islands?

10. What are Djibouti's two official languages? Hint: one is European.

11. What's Morocco's (non-alcoholic) national drink, jokingly known as 'Berber whisky'?

12. Is the Horn of Africa a peninsula, mountain or archipelago?

13. Gondar and Aksum are northern cities in which country?

14. What are the three main species of herbivores that undertake East Africa's Great Migration?

15. Known for its tropical beaches, on which island would you also find the Sir Seewoosagur Ramgoolam Botanical Garden?

16. What is the name given to people who originate from or live in Madagascar?

17. Which East African country is called the 'Land of 1,000 Hills'?

18. Which five colours feature on the Seychelles flag?

19. Can you name Ethiopia and Eritrea's fermented flatbread?

20. In which Southern African country would you find Mana Pools National Park?

21. If you visited Morocco, which currency would you need?

22. Which south-east African country bordered by Mozambique, Tanzania and Zambia has a large lake with the same name?

23. Which East African capital is widely known as the 'Cleanest City in Africa'?

24. Piton de la Fournaise and the capital Saint-Denis are two highlights on which Indian Ocean island?

25. At 4,167m tall, what is Morocco's highest mountain?

26. Lake Manyara and Tarangire are two wildlife parks in which country?

SOUTHERN & WESTERN AFRICA

1. Which of these Southern African countries is bigger by area: Botswana, Namibia or South Africa?

2. In which country would you find the pastel-pink Lake Retba?

3. Which Southern African country is known as the 'Kingdom of the Sky'?

4. Boulders Beach, South Africa is known as a hotspot for which species of penguin?

5. In which West African country is voodoo not only practiced but recognised by the country as an official religion?

6. Several African countries are named after rivers. Which is farthest west?

7. In Ghana, and across West Africa, *fufu* is an essential side dish to eat alongside stews. What are its two key ingredients?

8. Nana's Lodge offers off-the-beaten-track stays in which West African country?

9. How many major islands does Cape Verde have?

10. Which large aquatic mammal might you spot in Orango Islands National Park and Bissagos Island in Guinea-Bissau?

11. Do Niger and Nigeria share a border?

12. Which country has the bigger population: South Africa or Nigeria?

13. What's the number allocated to the most famous star dune at Sossusvlei in the Namib Desert?

14. What's the smallest country in mainland Southern Africa?

15. Which Southern African country has been dubbed 'Cheetah Capital of the World'?

16. Bo, Freetown and Kenema are the three largest cities in which country?

17. When in Sierra Leone, *poyo* is the drink of choice. What is it?

18. South Africa's pretty Cape Sugarbird can be found in which two of its provinces?

19. In which country is the Luangwa Valley, famous for its high density of wildlife, especially leopards?

20. The largest fetish market in the word is thought to be in Lomé, Togo. What is the market called?

21. South Africa's Garden Route, a coastal drive, is approximately how many kilometres long: 100, 300 or 700?

22. The country now called Eswatini was given its current name in 2018. What was it called before then?

23. African wild dogs, found in sub-Saharan Africa, are also called by which alternative name?

24. What is the world's second largest canyon (in Namibia) called?

25. The Mkgadikgadi in Botswana is a region of what – salt pans, sand dunes or volcanoes?

INDIA & SOUTH ASIA

1. Which South Asian country is bigger by area: Afghanistan or Pakistan?

2. In which South Asian country would you find Ari Atoll?

3. Which Nepalese town on the shore of Phewa Tal (Lake) is known as the 'Gateway to Annapurna'?

4. Karakoram is a mountain range in China and which four other South Asian countries?

5. In which Bhutanese valley would you find the important Buddhist monastery Gangtey?

6. Which three cities form India's popular Golden Triangle?

7. Bangladesh's UNESCO-listed Sompur Mahavihara was built in which century: 2nd, 8th or 16th?

8. In which Pakistani city would you find Wazir Khan Mosque?

9. On a visit to India, when you dip your hand into your purse, which currency will you pull out?

10. Lake Rara can be found in which South Asian country?

11. In which country would you find the Hunza Valley, known for its apples and beautiful mountainous scenery?

12. Kaziranga National Park in north-east India has incredible wildlife including the world's largest population of which endangered animal?

13. True cinnamon, also called Ceylon cinnamon, originates from which South Asian country?

14. Which country says that it measures success through 'Gross National Happiness'?

15. In which city will you find the magnificent Boudhanath Stupa?

16. Can you name both of Pakistan's official languages?

17. Roughly, how many Ajanta Caves are there in India: 20, 30 or 40?

18. Which island is dubbed 'the Galápagos of the Maldives'?

19. Can you name the Sri Lankan national park that is biggest by area? Hint: it isn't Yala.

20. Sri Kaileswaram Temple in Colombo, Sri Lanka is the oldest temple in the city... for which religion?

21. Dzongkha is the official language of which South Asian nation?

22. Nepal's Kathmandu Valley has three UNESCO-listed Durbar Squares. What does the name mean in English? And where are they?

23. In which Indian state would you be most likely to eat dhokla?

24. Jim Corbett National Park in India, one of the country's oldest, was created to protect which endangered species?

25. On which Sri Lankan coast is Negombo: east, north or west?

26. The image of Paro Taktsang temple embedded in a Bhutanese cliff face is iconic. What religion does the temple follow?

SOUTH-EAST ASIA

1. Is Borneo the largest island in all of Asia?

2. Which UNESCO-listed ancient site in Myanmar is known for its thousands of temples strewn across a wide plain?

3. Can you name at least one of the three gardens in Singapore's Gardens By The Bay?

4. How many South-East Asian countries have stars on their flags?

5. What is the name of the iconic towers of Kuala Lumpur, Malaysia?

6. In which South-East Asian country would you find the tiered Kuang Si Waterfall?

7. Which Vietnamese city has become known as the City of Bridges, thanks to its extraordinary Golden Hands Bridge, Dragon Bridge and several more unique constructions?

8. Kampong Ayer claims to be the world's biggest floating village with its own schools, mosques and restaurants. In which tiny nation is it?

9. In which Bali town would you find the Tegallalang Rice Terraces?

10. What is the name of Vietnam's popular national dish, made with rice noodles and broth?

11. Timor-Leste in South-East Asia is also known by what alternative name?

12. Koh Rong Island and glorious Long Beach are part of which South-East Asian country?

13. Palawan is pristine, and Boracay is popular. In which country would you find these places?

14. What is Bali's capital city?

15. Approximately how many temples can you find in the incredible Lao city of Luang Prabang: 30, 40 or 50?

16. In which country can you find the freshwater Inle Lake?

17. What is Ho Chi Minh City's former name?

18. The remains of Angkor Wat and Angkor Thom can be found near which modern day Cambodian city?

19. Can you name two of the three main Gili Islands in Indonesia?

20. Colugos are extraordinary animals. Are they birds, giant bats or gliding mammals?

21. What will you find in a hawker centre in Singapore?

22. In which South-East Asian country are the Atauro & Jaco Islands?

23. In which South-East Asian nation can you hike the Phousi Hills?

24. Which Filipino 'Queen City of the South' is known for its Spanish colonial architecture and surrounding islands?

25. A trip to Indonesia can offer a rare sighting of a Komodo dragon. How long do they typically live: 10, 20 or 30 years?

EAST ASIA

1. Which is bigger: South Korea, Japan or Mongolia?

2. In which South Korean city would you find Asia's largest seafood market, Jagalchi?

3. Fushimi Inari Taisha is a much-photographed red Shinto shrine in which Japanese city?

4. Which Chinese city is best known for its giant panda sanctuaries?

5. The largest desert in Asia is in East Asia. Can you name the desert and the countries it's in?

6. The 330m-tall Ryugyong Hotel looks like a pyramid. In which East Asian city would you find it?

7. In which Asian mountain range would you find the Potanin glacier?

8. If you were wandering down The Bund and Nanjing Road, in which East Asian city would you be in?

9. Japan's Aoshima Island is known for which adorable animal?

10. Mongolia has the world's second-biggest population of what type of rare, endangered big cat?

11. How many floors does the tallest tower in Taipei, Taiwan have – a number included in its name?

12. Which Japanese city is famous for the wild sika deer which roam through its namesake park?

13. Roughly how many people traverse Tokyo's Shibuya Crossing at any one time: 1,100, 2,500 or 3,800?

14. Ger is the Mongolian term for which kind of residence?

15. What is the key ingredient in tonkotsu ramen broth in Japan?

16. Snow monkeys, aka Japanese macaques, are often seen in Jigokudani Park on which Japanese island?

17. Known for its beautiful landscape and Paektamsa and Shinhungsa Buddhist temples, Mt Soraksan Nature Reserve is found in which country?

18. How many times is the letter 'a' used in the traditional spelling of Mongolia's capital city?

19. Which country allows only approved haircuts for its citizens?

20. Kawasaki, Japan has an annual festival during which penis-themed decorations are plentiful. What is it called?

21. Queues form at Lord Stow's Bakery in Macao for which Portuguese-style delicacy?

22. Which type of blossom do people flock to see in Japan each spring, which holds a very special place in the culture?

23. On which East Asian island would you find Sun Moon Lake?

24. Umbrellas, ready-made origami and work-ready ties can be bought in Japan's quirkiest vending machines. True or false?

25. Which truly unbelievable Chinese national park inspired the alien landscapes of the blockbuster film *Avatar* (2009)?

26. What's the name of the iconic passenger service that runs between Kowloon and Hong Kong Island?

AUSTRALIA & NEW ZEALAND

1. New Zealand has two major islands: North and South. Which is bigger by area?

2. Both Australia and New Zealand's flags feature the Union Jack, but which has more stars?

3. Mount Cook is New Zealand's South Island's most prominent mountain. What is its Maori name?

4. 50 million of what animal migrate across Christmas Island each year?

5. What's the name of the large and critically endangered flightless parrot found in New Zealand?

6. In which Australian states will you find these wine regions: Barossa Valley; Swan Valley; Hunter Valley?

7. What do you call the Maori method of cooking in a pit in the ground?

8. What is the world's smallest penguin species, which 'parades' each night on Australia's Phillip Island?

9. If there's one Aussie food you must try, it's Vegemite, a love-it-or-hate-it, dark, sticky spread. What is its main ingredient?

10. In which Australian state would you find the outback town of Coober Pedy?

11. Is New Zealand's Milford Sound an island, fjord or mountain?

12. *Lord of the Rings* film fans can visit the Hobbiton set near which New Zealand town?

13. This very unlikely Australian animal is sometimes described as a cross between a duck, a beaver and an otter – what is it?

14. New Zealand has three official languages, English included. One is culturally significant, and the other is accessible. Can you name them?

15. Which cool Kiwi city is known for its Sky Tower and a city park nestled inside a volcanic crater?

16. What is the scientific name for the natural phenomena known as the Southern Lights?

17. On which New South Wales bay can you swim with sea turtles at Julian Rocks?

18. Which Tasmanian mammal was reintroduced to the mainland in 2020?

19. The Routeburn, Abel Tasman and Milford are all what?

20. Which town in Australia's Northern Territory, named for the wife of a telegraph pioneer, is the main tourist hub for the Red Centre?

21. Rottnest Island, Western Australia, is best known as the home of which adorable, chubby-cheeked marsupial?

22. Can you name the steaming geyser in Rotorua, New Zealand?

23. There are more camels living wild in Arabia than in Outback Australia – true or false?

24. Who was Abel Tasman, the person for whom New Zealand's Abel Tasman National Park was named?

PACIFIC COUNTRIES

1. Not including Australia and New Zealand, what are the three key Pacific Islands regions, all ending in -esia?

2. In which Pacific nation is the popular wreck-diving site called Million Dollar Point?

3. Birdwatching haven Papua New Guinea is home to 760 species of birds, including birds-of-paradise. Roughly how many species of birds-of-paradise live there: 15, 29 or 40?

4. Which country is known for its 'cargo cults', one of which worships the Queen's husband, Prince Philip, as a divine being?

5. New Caledonia is a special territory of which European nation?

6. Palau's flag is yellow with a central blue circle. True or false?

7. Why isn't it safe to visit Bikini Atoll on the Marshall Islands?

8. Palusami is a popular dish in the Pacific Islands, made of corned beef, taro leaves and what kind of cream?

9. In which 'esia' is the photogenic island of Bora Bora?

10. In which Pacific nation is the Kalalin Pass coral reef?

11. Bungee jumping is believed to have developed from the 'land diving' undertaken by the men of Pentecost Island in which country?

12. How do you say 'hello' in Fijian?

13. *Kava* is a drink in Fiji and Tonga, as well as other Pacific nations. What exactly is kava, though?

14. In which Pacific country would you find the shipwrecked MS *World Discoverer* on Roderick Bay?

15. Which Micronesian archaeological site is sometimes called 'the Venice of the Pacific'?

16. Anibare Bay is just one of the natural highlights of which Pacific country?

17. The legendary Aggie Grey's Hotel was built in 1933, and notable guests have included Marlon Brando. In which country is it?

18. Which is the main international airport for Fiji?

19. Tok Pisin is an official language of which Pacific country?

20. The island of Guadalcanal is known for its World War II history, but in which Pacific country would you find it?

21. Is Tonga a kingdom or republic?

22. Funafuti Atoll is the capital of which small Pacific country?

23. Papua New Guinea occupies the eastern half of New Guinea Island. What is the western half called and which country is it part of?

24. Diving Chuuk Lagoon's shipwrecks is a Micronesia must-do. How many wrecks are there: around 40, 60 or 80?

25. Ha'amonga 'a Maui Trilithon is a 13th-century stone wonder located in which Pacific country?

26. Which sport is the national sport of Fiji, and is popular through much of the region?

UNITED STATES OF AMERICA

1. In which US state would you find the Grand Canyon?

2. How many of the USA's 50 states does the Mississippi River run through or border?

3. The faces of which four US presidents are carved into South Dakota's Mount Rushmore?

4. In which state can you find the Everglades?

5. Which US national park is the oldest?

6. What's the name of the erstwhile home of Elvis Presley, now a museum, in Memphis, Tennessee?

7. How tall is Seattle's famous Space Needle (spire included): 101m, 184m or 260m?

8. Salt Lake City is the capital of which US state?

9. Thousands of what type of whale congregate off Maui, Hawaii, each year, making it a whale-watching Mecca?

10. You'll find a Kansas City in both Kansas and Missouri. In which state would you find the famous Joe's Kansas City Bar-B-Que restaurant?

11. New York's Central Park is bigger than which two countries of the world?

12. On which Michigan island would you find a Butterfly House, Skull Cave and the limestone Arch Rock?

13. The Golden Gate Bridge in San Francisco was painted a useful colour. Can you name the exact shade?

14. In which state would you find the dramatic, towering dunes of Great Sand Dunes National Park?

15. Alcatraz Island in California was a working prison until which year: 1963, 1979 or 1995?

16. In which US valley would you find the striking orange rock formation called the Ear of the Wind?

17. Hana Highway is the ultimate road trip along the coast of which Hawaiian island?

18. In Chicago, trying deep-dish pizza is essential. Traditionally, in which order do the cheese, tomato sauce and toppings go?

19. Does the US have an official national language?

20. Boston is one of the USA's best-loved cities. Which state is it in?

21. There are two major cities called Portland in the USA. One is in Oregon. Where is the other?

22. In which Alaskan city can you learn about indigenous people at the Native Heritage Centre?

23. In which mountain range would you find the volcano Mount Rainier?

24. Cumberland Island in Georgia is known for its abundance of which animal?

25. Which species of eagle is the symbol of the USA?

26. In which US city and state can you (metaphorically) ring the Liberty Bell?

CANADA

1. What's the affectionate nickname for Canadians, ending in 'ck'?

2. Canada shares a border with Alaska. True or false?

3. Newfoundland and Labrador – Canada's easternmost province – are also the names of two breeds of dog. True or false?

4. What is Canada's oldest national park? It's one of the best known.

5. What is the plural noun for moose?

6. On which Canadian island can you visit the Green Gables house and farm, setting for the book *Anne of Green Gables*?

7. Montmorency Falls and the Plains of Abraham can be found in which Canadian city?

8. The Nova Scotia donair is a regional speciality of which late-night food: pizza, kebab or sandwich?

9. What's the favourite Canadian dish of fries, cheese curds and gravy called?

10. How many waterfalls make up Niagara Falls, and which of the falls is the biggest?

11. Iqaluit and Auyuittuq National Park are found in which Arctic Canadian territory?

12. Montreal, Quebec City and Edmonton are three predominantly French-speaking Canadian cities. True or false?

13. Two-thirds of the world's population of which white whale spends its summer in Canadian waters?

14. In which famous mountain range would you find the Athabasca Glacier?

15. Which remote town on Hudson Bay is dubbed the 'Polar Bear Capital of the World'?

16. The architecturally unusual Royal Art Museum is made of which shape: domes, prisms or rectangles?

17. In which Canadian province can you drive the scenic Icefields Parkway to the UNESCO-listed Jasper National Park?

18. Casa Loma, a grand mansion and garden, can be found in which Canadian city?

19. How many species of bear are found in Canada?

20. Banff National Park's best-known lake shares a woman's name. Do you know what it is?

21. On which British Columbian bay would you find The Butchart Gardens?

22. Grouse Mountain, Queen Elizabeth Park and the Capilano Suspension Bridge are all in which Canadian city?

23. What is the name of the luxury train service that runs from Vancouver on a choice of three routes?

24. Is Granville Island in Vancouver an island or a peninsula?

25. Which Canadian bay, lying between Nova Scotia and New Brunswick, has the highest tides on Earth?

26. Of which Canadian Territory is Whitehorse capital?

MEXICO &
THE CARIBBEAN

1. Which Caribbean country is bigger by area: Dominican Republic or Anguilla?

2. In which Mexican city can you eat local at Mercado de Benito Juarez and enjoy the Guelaguetza Festival?

3. Morne Trois Pitons is a UNESCO-inscribed national park in which Caribbean country?

4. Willemstad is the colourful, Amsterdam-esque capital of which Caribbean island?

5. Trendy Tulum is located on which Mexican peninsula?

6. Which North American country has the biggest population: Mexico or Canada?

7. Is Trinidad & Tobago the northernmost or southernmost Caribbean island country?

8. What is the Jamaican dish of *callaloo*?

9. In which Caribbean territory would you find the luminous blue bay Bahía Bioluminiscente?

10. Punta Sur Reef is a dive site off which Mexican island?

11. Stingray City is an area of shallow sandbars where you can snorkel, wade or dive with stingrays (please be responsible). Where is it?

12. In which Caribbean country could you visit the famous River Antoine Rum Distillery and see chocolate production at the Belmont Estate?

13. Puebla, a city in Mexico, is known for which type of tile?

14. Yucatán, Mexico is known for thousands of sinkholes or underwater caves, many of which make natural swimming pools. What is the name given to them?

15. Is Anguilla an overseas territory of the United Kingdom, France or the Netherlands?

16. In which Mexican city would you find the awe-inspiring pink spire of Parroquia de San Miguel Arcángel church?

17. Uxmal is a historically important ancient city built by which civilisation?

18. What is the full official name of the Caribbean nation known as St Kitts & Nevis?

19. Traditional tequila is made from which plant?

20. What is the collective name given to the series of spectacular canyons that run through the Sierra Madre in north-western Mexico?

21. Carriacou, a laidback, little-visited island, is part of which country?

22. Can you name the largest city of Guadeloupe, a French territory in the Caribbean?

23. Sans-Souci Palace was built in the 19th century for which Haitian monarch?

CENTRAL AMERICA

1. How many countries are there in Central America (officially)?

2. Which Central American country has the biggest population?

3. What bird with a multi-coloured beak and bright yellow chest is the national bird of Belize?

4. Honduras shares a border with three Central American countries. Which are they?

5. El Salvador is the smallest of the Central American countries by sq km. True or false?

6. How many national parks does Costa Rica have: 7, 30 or 56?

7. Nicaragua has two Corn Islands, both named for their size. Can you name them both?

8. What's the colloquial term for a native of Costa Rica?

9. Which primates, several species of which are found in Central America, are believed to be among the loudest on earth?

10. In which Central American country can you enjoy a flower-filled walk along the Ruta de las Flores?

11. *Baleadas* are made of flour tortillas, mashed fried beans, salty cheese and mantequilla cream. In which Central American country would you mostly likely try one?

12. Panamá Viejo is the ruin which was once part of which Panamanian city?

13. Which country has the second longest coral reef in the world?

14. Is Costa Rica's incredible Monteverde Cloud Forest Reserve towards the north or south of the country?

15. Are caimans reptiles, mammals or amphibians?

16. What is Nicaragua's currency, which shares its name with both a Spanish and Argentinian city?

17. The tiered, turquoise pools of natural wonder Semuc Champey are hidden in which Central American country?

18. In which Central American country could you visit Cerro Verde volcano and the pretty city of Santa Ana?

19. How many stars are on the flag of Honduras?

20. *Pepián* is a Guatemalan dish with a bit of a kick, usually made with which meat?

21. Which national park is home to Honduras's highest peak, Cerro Las Minas?

22. Central America is known for its excellent coffee. Which country produces the most coffee?

23. The Mayan ruins of El Tazumal can be found in which Central American country?

24. Guatemala is home to Central America's tallest volcano. What is it called?

25. Which lake, the largest in Central America, is home to a population of sharks, despite being freshwater?

26. In which country would you find the archaeological site of Lamanai, once a large Maya city?

SOUTH AMERICA

1. Which South American city is biggest by area: Rio de Janeiro, Bogotá or La Paz?

2. The 67m-high Obelisco, a striking white monument built in the 1930s, stands tall in which South American city?

3. The Andean condor is the national bird of Chile, Colombia and Ecuador. True or false?

4. For which political and military figure is Venezuela's official title and currency named?

5. The Salt Cathedral of Zipaquirá is underground in which nation?

6. Paulista Avenue and Ibirapuera Park are two important sites in which Brazilian city?

7. What's the name of Bolivia's famous mirror-like salt pan – the world's largest?

8. In which Chilean desert is Valle de la Luna (Valley of the Moon)?

9. Spanish is the main official language of Peru. What are the two next most widely spoken tongues?

10. Quirky attractions such as the Devil Tooth peak, Coca Museum and Witches' Market are found in which South American city?

11. Which South American country is most closely connected to the legend of El Dorado?

12. The world's largest rodent roams freely in the wilds of South America. Do you know its name?

13. Parsley, salt, wine vinegar and garlic are ingredients of which green Argentinian/Uruguayan sauce, often served with grilled meat?

14. What is the official language of Brazil?

15. In which South American country can you visit Stabroek Market and Rewa Eco-Lodge?

16. Actress Eva Perón's grave can be visited in which Argentinian cemetery?

17. Monday's Falls cascade in which South American country?

18. The Mitad del Mundo (Middle of the World) near Quito is a monument to the equator. True or false?

19. What do a town in Bolivia, a famous beach in Rio de Janeiro and a Barry Manilow song all have in common?

20. There are an estimated 12,000 of which type of penguin on Chile's Magdalena Island?

21. Which two South American countries have a Fort Zeelandia?

22. What is the highest peak in South America?

23. In which South American territory can you visit the quiet beach of Plages de Montjoly?

24. The popular cities of Cusco and Trujillo belong to which South American country?

25. In Valparaíso, Chile, you can visit a museum which is the former home of which Nobel Prize-winning poet?

26. Which Brazilian city is known for its coastal charm, pastel-hued colonial architecture and the Elevador Lacerda lift?

THE ANTARCTIC & NEARBY ISLANDS

1. Most Antarctic cruises leave from which Argentinian city, sometimes called 'The City at the End of the World'?

2. Can you name the largest ice shelf in Antarctica?

3. Is Antarctica technically classed as a national park?

4. To the nearest degree, can you guess the coldest temperature ever recorded in Antarctica? -48°C, -89°C or -98°C ?

5. On which Antarctic archipelago would you find the mountainous Elephant Island?

6. Can you name two of the six types of seal found in the Antarctic?

7. Where in Antarctica is home to a unique, UK-style, penguin-surrounded post office?

8. Which penguin, endemic to Antarctica, is the largest?

9. Kodak Gap is the nickname for which scenic, mountainous Antarctic channel?

10. McMurdo Station is one of the most well-known research stations in Antarctica. To which country does it belong?

11. The Arctic tern, also called the sea swallow, migrates from the northern hemisphere to the Antarctic each year. True or false?

12. Sailing past Paradise Bay's icebergs and ice floes is a dream. But can you step foot on Antarctica here?

13. Does Antarctica have an official time zone?

14. Deception Island has a unique shape as well as an unusual name. Which shape is it: heart, triangle or horseshoe?

15. Is the continent of Antarctica double, triple or quadruple the size of Australia?

16. What is the primary colour of the snow petrel, one of few birds seen in Antarctica?

17. Antarctica is home to hundreds of subglacial lakes. Can you name the biggest and most famous?

18. What indigenous people used to live on Antarctica?

19. What is the capital of the Falkland Islands, often visited on cruises to the Antarctic?

20. To the nearest kilometre, how thick is the ice on the South Pole: one, two or three km?

21. Princess Martha Coast flanks the Weddell Sea. To which European royal family did Princess Martha belong?

22. You can see orcas, sperm whales, humpback and southern right whales in Antarctica. True or false?

23. Which penguin species has the biggest population in the Antarctic?

24. Is Erebus a mountain, volcano or glacier in the Antarctic?

25. South Georgia is another common Antarctic cruise destination. It is an overseas territory of which country?

26. Vindication and Revenge are two islands in the South Sandwich archipelago, a common Antarctic cruise stop. True or false?

WHERE IN THE WORLD

Geography nerds and map devotees rejoice, for this collection of tricky quizzes is for you!

This chapter will take you on overland journeys across borders, and on expeditions through autonomous and disputed territories. You'll whizz through the world's capital cities, and try to identify outlines of continents, countries and even the world's flags. Test your knowledge of the people that make each country unique, and explore fascinating cultural and religious festivals.

Can you navigate this tough trivia, or is your knowledge borderline? Can you work out cleverly worded co-ordinate clues, or will you need a compass? Time to find out.

MATCH THE CONTINENTS

Match the outlines with the continents: Africa, Asia, North America, South America, Europe, Oceania (Australia) and Antarctica. Enjoy!

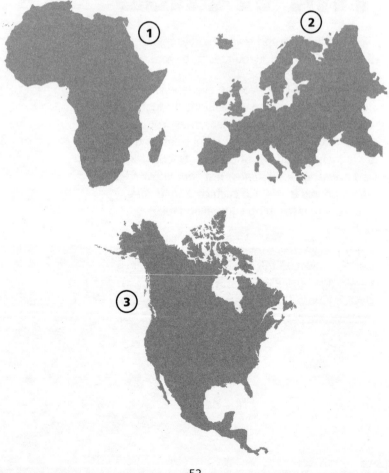

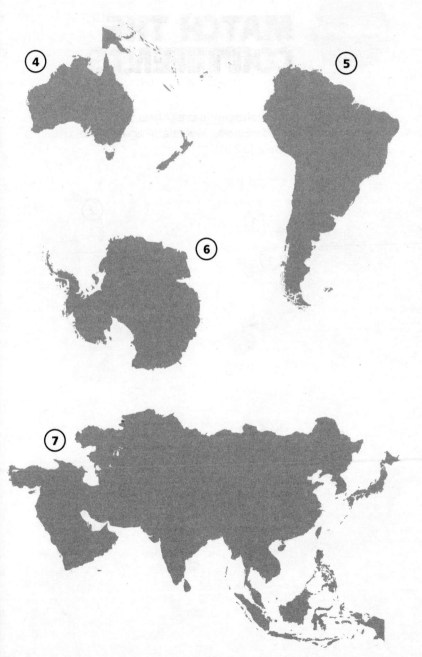

MATCH THE COUNTRIES

Can you match up these outlines to the correct country? Here are your options: Italy, Mongolia, Namibia, Uruguay, Finland, Argentina, Kazakhstan and Peru.

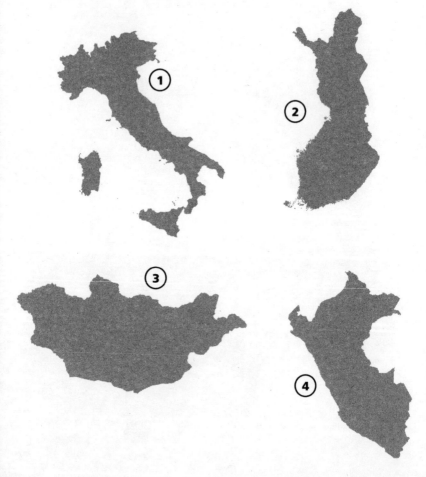

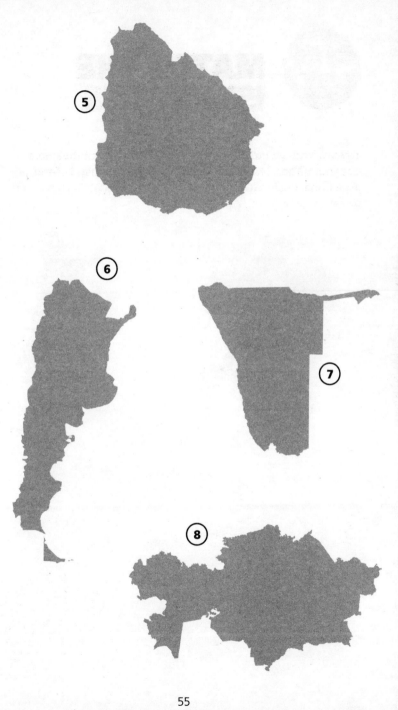

MATCH THE ISLANDS

Which island is which? Match Borneo, Isle of Skye (Scotland), Kangaroo Island (Australia), South Georgia, Greenland, Tavarua (Fiji), Isabela Island (Galápagos) and Palm Jumeirah in Dubai to the correct outline.

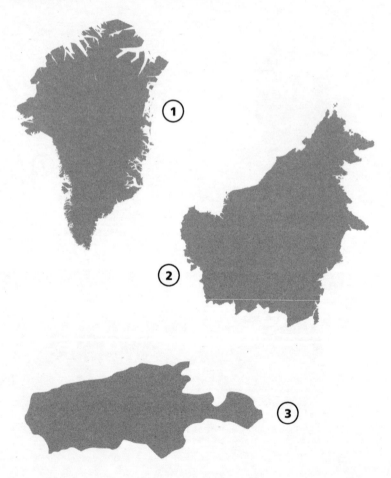

56

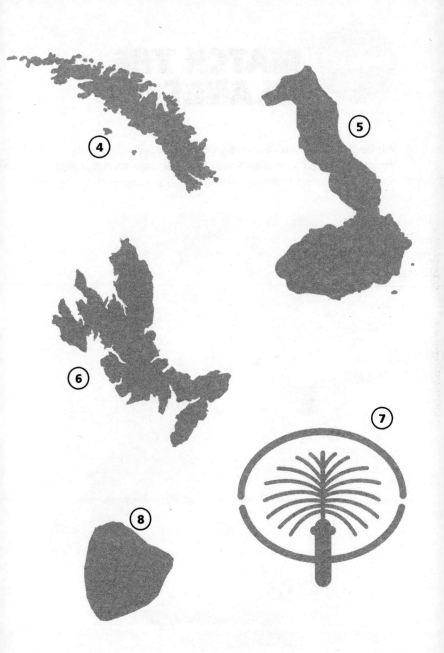

MATCH THE US STATES

Alaska, Ohio, Florida, Maryland, California, Hawaii, Texas and Tennessee all have recognisable shapes, but can you match them up to their correct outline? Good luck!

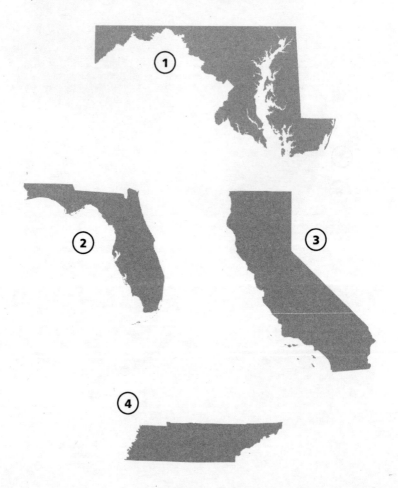

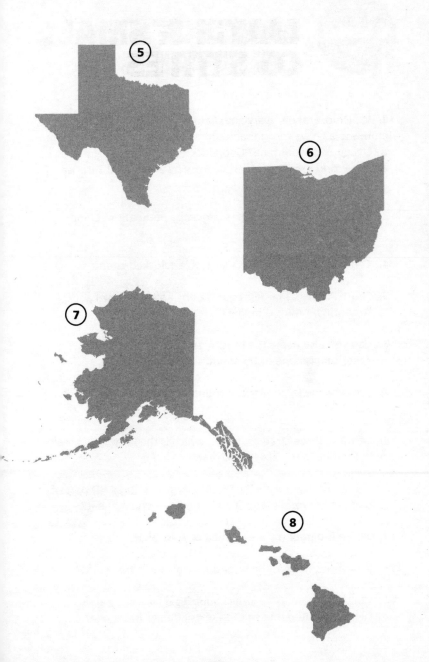

LARGE & SMALL COUNTRIES

1. Which country is the world's largest by area: is it Russia, China or India?

2. The world's second largest country by area might surprise you. Have a guess...

3. Which of these countries is largest by population: China, Brazil or Pakistan?

4. Can you name the world's largest landlocked country?

5. South America's largest countries by area are Brazil and Argentina. Which is bigger?

6. Can you also name the third-biggest country in South America, also one of the world's largest?

7. Which is the larger African country by area: Libya, Algeria or Sudan?

8. Of these three large countries, which is the largest by area: Indonesia, Mexico or Kazakhstan?

9. This island territory is the world's largest island AND part of one of the world's largest countries. Can you name it?

10. Which is bigger (by area): India or Australia?

11. Which country has the largest capital city in the world?

12. Which of these three large countries is largest by area: Democratic Republic of the Congo, Iran or Mongolia?

13. Can you name the world's smallest country by area? Hint: It's in Europe

14. Now, which country is the world's smallest by population?

15. These three countries are among Europe's smallest. Which is the biggest: Montenegro, Luxembourg or Andorra?

16. Which country is officially Africa's smallest by area? Hint: think islands...

17. How about the smallest African mainland country by area: Rwanda, Djibouti or The Gambia?

18. Do you know the smallest Caribbean country by area? Hint: think two islands...

19. How about Central America's smallest country by area?

20. Can you identify South America's smallest country by area: Suriname, Guyana or Ecuador?

21. Singapore is often thought to be Asia's smallest country by area, but it's actually...?

22. What is the smallest Pacific Island nation by area? Hint: It begins with the letter 'N'.

23. Exactly how tiny do you think that Pacific Island nation is? Is it 21, 31 or 41 sq km?

24. Which of these four small countries is smallest by area: Tonga, Bahrain, Samoa or the Federated States of Micronesia?

25. Which country has the smallest capital city in the world?

26. Which of these three small countries is smallest by area: Saint Vincent and the Grenadines, Malta or Grenada?

CO-ORDINATES & CLUES

1. At 90.0000° S, 45.0000° E, you'll have gone where few explorers get to go, at a unique southern point on the surface of the Earth. Where are you?

2. At 29.9773° N, 31.1325° E, you'll be looking up in awe at three notably triangular monuments. Where are you?

3. At 19.8206° N, 155.4681° W, you'll be on a stunning island, looking up at the world's tallest mountain from base to summit. Where are you?

4. At 90.0000° N, 135.0000° W, you'll be as far north as one can ever travel. Where are you?

5. At 44.2440° N, 7.7693° E, you'll uncover a popular Google Earth gem: an enormous pink... what? And where?

6. At 40.7484° N; 73.9857° W, you'll be feeling rather dizzy as you ascend this very famous American city's iconic, 102-storey skyscraper. Where are you?

7. At 0.1807° S, 78.4678° W, you'll be approximately 22km from the equator in one of South America's most fascinating cities, high in the Andes. Where are you?

8. At 14.0222° N, 120.9839° E, you'll be experiencing another Google Earth oddity – looking at a lake on an island, which is surrounded by a lake. And another island. Where are you?

9. At 18.7669° S, 46.8691° E, you'll be in the middle of a lemur-loving island, on the Tropic of Capricorn. Where are you?

10. At 51.4769° N, 0.0005° W, you'll be at the British location where you can stand on the Prime Meridian. Where are you?

11. At 27.1127° S, 109.3497° W, you'll be puzzling over the mysterious moai head statues on a remote island. Where are you?

12. At 25.3444° S, 131.0369° E, you'll be admiring the most famous red monolith of this Oceanian country's Northern Territory. Where are you?

13. At 41.6488° N, 0.8891° W, you'll be preparing to explore a UNESCO-listed city in Europe home to Aljafería Palace and a Prime Meridian connection. Where are you?

14. At 48.8867° N, 2.3431° E, you'll be stood at a famous white hilltop church in the French capital. Where are you?

15. At 51.1789° N, 1.8262° W, you'll be in southern England, visiting an iconic UNESCO site – one of the world's most impressive and mysterious standing stone landmarks. Where are you?

16. At 82.5018° N, 62.3481° W, you'll be at the northernmost inhabited place on Earth. You'll also be pretty cold. Where are you?

17. At 46.4179° S, 168.3615° E, you'll be standing somewhere in the southernmost city of a far-south country known for its North and South Islands. Where are you?

18. At 38.7223° N, 9.1393° W, you'll be exploring a sunny, coastal European capital known for its old-school trams and blue-and-white tiles. Where are you?

19. At 0°N 0°E, you'll be adrift in the middle of an ocean, at the exact point where something unique happens. Where are you?

ON THE BORDER

1. Can you name the two landlocked countries in South America?

2. Brazil shares a border with every South American country bar two. Do you know which two?

3. Are there any landlocked countries in Central America?

4. Does the South American country of Peru share a border with Chile, Colombia and Ecuador?

5. Argentina shares a border with Chile, Paraguay and Uruguay. True or false?

6. How many countries share a border with China – 9, 12, or 14?

7. Can you name at least four countries that border China?

8. Does Uzbekistan share a border with Tajikistan, Turkmenistan and Azerbaijan?

9. Can you name one of the four countries that shares a border with Georgia?

10. Is Sri Lanka a landlocked country in Asia?

11. Can you name at least two of the seven countries that border India?

12. Can you name the three countries that each share a border with five Indian states?

13. Is Laos a landlocked country in South-East Asia?

14. How many countries share a border with Russia? It's in double figures.

15. Can you name at least three countries that border Russia?

16. How many landlocked countries are there in Europe? There are more than ten but fewer than 20

17. How many countries share a border with Germany?

18. Can you name at least three of Germany's border countries? It's as easy as A, B, C

19. Firstly, do you know how many countries share a border with Croatia?

20. Now, can you go one better and name one country that shares a border with Croatia?

21. Norway is bordered by three countries. Can you name all three?

22. Does Denmark share a border with Sweden?

23. Can you guess how many landlocked countries there are in Africa?

24. Is Botswana a landlocked country, bordered by Namibia and South Africa (among others)?

25. Kenya, known as Jamhuri ya Kenya in Swahili, shares a border with Ethiopia and Tanzania. Correct?

26. The Southern African countries of Zambia and Zimbabwe do not share a border. True or false?

UNIQUE PASSPORTS

1. In which century was the concept of a passport first mentioned?

2. According to the Henley Passport Index 2020 (which notes how many countries each nationality can visit visa-free), which nation's passport is the most powerful?

3. So, how many countries do you think passport holders from that nation can visit without a visa – 91, 151 or 191?

4. According to the same index, which nation's passport is the second most powerful?

5. According to the same index, which European nation's passport is the most powerful?

6. According to the same index, which nation's passport is the least powerful in the world?

7. According to the same index, which nation's passport is more powerful: UK, US or Australian?

8. Passports can come in different shades of which four colours?

9. Do you know the colour of the USA's standard passport?

10. Is it true that the Australia passport features an image of a kangaroo?

11. Finland's passport has a flick-book cartoon in the corners of its pages, featuring which animal?

12. Is it true that the Northern Lights are depicted inside the pages of a post-2014 Norwegian passport?

13. People don't just have passports in the UAE, individual birds of a type of raptor do, too. Which type of bird?

14. What colour are the passports belonging to the majority of Peruvian citizens?

15. Is it true that the Canadian passport front cover features an image of Queen Elizabeth II?

16. Which country's former passport design featured the image of a breastfeeding woman?

17. Japanese passports have which flower on the front?

18. What does Easter Island's unique passport stamp look like?

19. The sleekly-designed Swiss passport features an abundance of which symbol?

20. Egypt's general passport design is an unusual shade of which colour?

21. Following the country's exit from the EU, the UK passport changed colour as of mid-2020. Which colour is it now?

22. Is it true that you'll find the Komodo dragon and rafflesia flower within the pages of Indonesia's passport?

23. What colour is New Zealand's passport and the writing on it?

24. Is it true you can get your passport stamped at Machu Picchu?

25. Each state gets its own page of Mexico's standard passport. How many Mexican states are there?

AUTONOMOUS & DISPUTED STATES

1. Madeira and the Azores are autonomous regions of which European country?

2. Which disputed region is known as the 'Roof of the World'?

3. In which country would you find the autonomous region of Vojvodina?

4. Home to Noah's Mausoleum, which exclave of Azerbaijan has declared itself an autonomous republic?

5. Zanzibar is a semi-autonomous region of which country?

6. At time of going to press, Bougainville is not yet independent. Is it an autonomous city, island cluster or district in Papua New Guinea?

7. Karelia has a long history with Finland, Sweden, Russia and Norway. Specifically, where would you find the autonomous Republic of Karelia today?

8. The beautiful islands of the Azores archipelago are in the Atlantic, approximately how far from Portugal – 900, 1,100 or 1,600 km?

9. What is the official name for Taiwan used by the ruling government on the island?

10. Northern Cyprus is recognised by the international community as part of the Republic of Cyprus. Which country recognises it as an independent country?

11. Which region of northern Greece, famous for its monasteries, has autonomous status?

12. Hong Kong has long been a 'special administrative region' of China, but which currency is used there?

13. Which other 'special administrative region' of China lies across the estuary of the Pearl River?

14. The autonomous Åland Islands sit in the Baltic Sea and the locals speak Swedish. But which country do they belong to?

15. The Faroe Islands governs itself, though remains part of which European kingdom?

16. In which recent year did Kosovo declare its independence from Serbia – 2008, 2009 or 2010?

17. In which autonomous region of China would you find the city of Ordos and the Mausoleum of Genghis Khan?

18. South Tyrol has three official languages, the most commonly spoken being German. Which country is it a province of?

19. Katuaq Cultural Centre and the Church of our Saviour are just two attractions in which capital city of an autonomous region of Denmark?

20. Artsakh (Nagorno-Karabakh) has declared itself a republic, but the international community recognises it as part of which country?

21. Which autonomous region of France has Italian influences, its native tongue is a type of Italian, and it was birthplace of a famous emperor?

22. The Soviet-style, self-declared nation of Transnistria makes for a fascinating visit. What is its capital city?

UNINHABITED PLACES

Wanderlust

1. To which country do the uninhabited Antipodes Islands belong?

2. Bouvet, an uninhabited dependency of Norway, holds the Guinness World Record for being the world's remotest... what?

3. What percentage of Canada is uninhabited – 60 or 80%?

4. The Bahamas island Big Major Cay is overrun with which farmyard animal?

5. The British Overseas Territory of Pitcairn Island isn't completely devoid of people. How small is the population: up to 50, between 51 and 100, or higher?

6. Which Alaskan city is often called 'the town under one roof', as most of its circa 200 residents live in the same building?

7. In which ocean would you find the uninhabited coral atoll Clipperton Island?

8. Antarctica is uninhabited on a permanent basis by people. Regardless, does it have any cities?

9. The Atlantic island of Tristan da Cunha has a tiny population of fewer than 300 people. What is their primary language?

10. Ball's Pyramid, part of the Lord Howe Island group in Australia, is an uninhabited...?

11. How many of the 145 islands and rocks comprising the Isles of Scilly are inhabited by people?

12. Ilha da Queimada Grande in Brazil is designated off-limits to the public in order to protect what creatures?

13. Can you name the largest uninhabited island in the world, and the country it belongs to?

14. What volcano is at the heart of the 'Valley of Death' on Russia's Kamchatka Peninsula?

15. Another unsurprisingly empty Death Valley, on the border of the Great Basin Desert, can be found in which US state?

16. In which country would you find the mysterious, uninhabited island of Spinalonga?

17. Which population-free Scottish island is the UK's only dual UNESCO World Heritage Site?

18. How far away from the nearest mainland is the scarcely populated Ascension Island – 1,000, 1,600 or 2,000 km?

19. Is Kabwe, the Zambian town often called 'the world's most toxic', uninhabited?

20. Hatutu Nature Reserve covers the entire uninhabited Hatutu Island. Which island group is it part of?

21. Why is Plymouth, the capital of Montserrat, completely uninhabited?

22. Which French Polynesian archipelago is Disappointment Island part of?

23. Which deserted California mining town shares its name with a type of three-coloured cat?

24. Glenrio, a ghost town on the border of New Mexico and Texas, can be found along which historic driving route?

PEOPLE OF THE WORLD

Wanderlust

1. 'Scousers' is the nickname given to people born in which English city?

2. When is International Day of the World's Indigenous Peoples each year?

3. Approximately how many uncontacted tribes are believed to survive across the world – around 30, around 75 or around 100?

4. In which African country would you meet the tribes who live alongside the Omo Valley?

5. Do you know the name of the fur hats worn by Kazakh eagle hunters?

6. In which country would you find the indigenous Kayapo peoples?

7. The Inca civilisation of South America thrived from the 13th century, until it was wiped out in which century?

8. From where did the affectionate nickname 'Kiwi' for New Zealander originate?

9. What is the meaning of the word Wodaabe, the name of an African tribe?

10. The Maasai ethnic group live in which two East African countries?

11. In which Papua New Guinea village could you watch the Baining fire dancers perform?

12. In Iceland, surnames end in either son or dóttir. Do you know the rule for determining who gets which surname?

13. Which indigenous people were the original residents of Japan's northern island, Hokkaido?

14. The Huli wigmen of Papua New Guinea not only ceremoniously grow their hair out, but also paint their faces in sacred ambua clay. Which colour is it?

15. Navajo peoples originate from which part of the USA: south-western, north-western or south-eastern?

16. The majority of Maya descendants today live in which Central American country? Hint: It's where the Maya site Tikal is...

17. Torres Strait Islanders are indigenous peoples from which country?

18. Gauchos, llaneros and huasos are all types of what?

19. Japan's Ama divers are mostly women who dive to find... what?

20. In Japan who or what is a *maiko*?

21. The Sámi people of Arctic Finland and Russia traditionally make a living by herding which animal?

22. Can you name the inspiring and energetic ceremonial dance performed by the Maori people of New Zealand?

23. Women of the Suri tribe in Ethiopia wear what on (or in) their lips as a mark of beauty?

24. In which Central American country will you find the Garifuna people?

CULTURAL & RELIGIOUS FESTIVALS

Wanderlust

1. On which day is Mexico's annual celebration Cinco de Mayo celebrated each year?

2. India's joyous Holi Festival is often called the festival of what: colour, light or autumn?

3. What is the name of Thailand's New Year Festival, in which locals soak each other with water pistols?

4. In which African countries do the Wodaabe people stage the Gerewol courtship festival?

5. In which country is the Goroka Show, which includes displays by various tribes including the Mudmen of Asaro?

6. The Guatemala Kite Festival fills the sky with giant, multi-coloured kites on which significant day each year?

7. The town of Haro, Spain is known for its sticky summer festival. What do its participants throw at each other?

8. What's the name of the Tibetan New Year festival celebrated in Bhutan, India and Nepal?

9. Do you know which year the Notting Hill Carnival, a celebration of Caribbean culture in London, first began?

10. Which 'three games of men' are played during Mongolia's traditional Naadam Festival?

11. The Bahamas' annual Junkanoo parades are always vivacious, but where would you visit to find the largest?

12. Inti Raymi, a yearly religious festival celebrated in Cusco, Peru is devoted to which Inca god?

13. Diwali, the Hindu Festival of Lights, lasts for how many days?

14. Which annual festival in Bhutan celebrates the arrival of a sacred bird?

15. Hornbill Festival celebrates and preserves the culture of the tribes living in which Indian state?

16. On which Venice waterway does the annual Regata Storica boat race take place?

17. The UNESCO-listed, 700-year-old Catholic parade in Bruges, Belgium is called the Procession of the Holy... what?

18. Colombia's Feria de Flores is known for its floral displays, but it also features the world's biggest parade of which animal?

19. The week-long Maslenitsa Festival sees Russians feast on which sweet food?

20. Up Helly Aa, a fiery, torch-lit procession, takes place on which Scottish archipelago?

21. Vesak Day celebrates the birth, enlightenment and death of which revered spiritual leader?

22. The Carnival of Oruro features dramatic masks and folk dances. In which country would you find Oruro?

23. There are two key lantern-releasing festivals in Taiwan. One is historic, the other is mainly for visitors. Can you name the historic festival?

24. Which incredible Chinese ice and snow festival is the largest in the world?

CAPITAL CITIES OF ASIA & THE PACIFIC

Wanderlust

1. What is the capital of Nepal?

2. What is the capital of Vietnam?

3. What is the capital of New Zealand?

4. What is the capital of Cambodia?

5. What is the capital of Uzbekistan?

6. What is the capital of South Korea?

7. What is the capital of the Maldives?

8. What is the capital of Pakistan?

9. Dushanbe is the capital of which country?

10. What is the capital of Laos?

11. What is the capital of Papua New Guinea?

12. What is the capital of Australia?

13. What is the capital of Myanmar (Burma)?

14. What is the capital of Afghanistan?

15. Nur-Sultan is the capital of which country?

16. What is the capital of Kyrgyzstan?

17. What is the capital of Turkmenistan?

18. What is the capital of China?

19. What is the capital of Thailand?

20. What is the capital of Bangladesh?

21. What is the capital of India?

22. What is the capital of the Philippines?

23. Beirut is the capital of which country?

24. What is the capital of Turkey?

25. What is the capital of Brunei?

26. What is the capital of Bhutan?

CAPITAL CITIES OF AFRICA

1. What is the capital of Ghana?

2. Kampala is the capital of which country?

3. What is the capital of Malawi?

4. What is the capital of Morocco?

5. South Africa officially has three different capitals. Which cities are they?

6. Antananarivo is the capital of which country?

7. What is the capital of Zambia?

8. Which country's two capitals are Mbabane and Lobamba?

9. What is the capital of the Seychelles?

10. What is the capital of Lesotho?

11. What is the capital of Rwanda?

12. What is the capital of Tunisia?

13. What is the capital of Sierra Leone?

14. Monrovia is the capital of which country?

15. What is the capital of Kenya?

16. What is the capital of Zimbabwe?

17. What is the current capital of Tanzania? It's not as obvious as you might think!

18. Gaborone is the capital of which country?

19. What is the capital of Comoros?

20. What is the capital of São Tomé and Príncipe?

21. N'Djamena is the capital of which country?

22. What is the capital of Mauritius?

23. What is the capital of Cabo Verde?

24. Banjul is the capital of which country?

25. What is the capital of Ethiopia?

26. What is the capital of the Democratic Republic of the Congo?

CAPITAL CITIES OF EUROPE

1. What is the capital of Estonia?

2. What is the capital of Greece?

3. What is the capital of Albania?

4. What is the capital of Armenia?

5. What is the capital of Luxembourg?

6. Sarajevo is the capital of which country?

7. What is the capital of Poland?

8. What is the capital of Spain?

9. What is the capital of Bulgaria?

10. Ljubljana is the capital of which country?

11. What is the capital of Norway?

12. What is the capital of Portugal?

13. What is the capital of Moldova?

14. What is the capital of Romania?

15. Tbilisi is the capital of which country?

16. What is the capital of Liechtenstein?

17. What is the capital of Austria?

18. What is the capital of Ukraine?

19. What is the capital of Azerbaijan?

20. Zagreb is the capital of which country?

21. What is the capital of Belarus?

22. What is the capital of Malta?

23. What is the capital of Ireland?

24. What is the capital of Iceland?

25. What is the capital of Andorra?

26. What is the capital of Montenegro?

CAPITALS CITIES OF THE AMERICAS

1. What is the capital of Nicaragua?

2. What is the capital of Bolivia?

3. What is the capital of Ecuador?

4. What is the capital of Brazil?

5. Caracas is the capital of which country?

6. What is the capital of El Salvador?

7. What is the capital of Canada?

8. What is the capital of Trinidad and Tobago?

9. What is the capital of Dominican Republic?

10. What is the capital of Colombia?

11. Paramaribo is the capital of which country?

12. What is the capital of Guyana?

13. What is the capital of Peru?

14. What is the capital of the United States of America?

15. Port-au-Prince is the capital of which country?

16. What is the capital of Mexico?

17. What is the capital of Chile?

18. What is the capital of Argentina?

19. What is the capital of Jamaica?

20. What is the capital of Barbados?

21. Asunción is the capital of which country?

22. What is the capital of Dominica?

23. What is the capital of Panama?

24. What is the capital of Costa Rica?

25. What is the capital of Honduras?

26. What is the capital of Uruguay?

MATCH THE FLAG OUTLINES

Can you match the flag to the country by just its outline, with no colour? Choose from: South Korea, Seychelles, Canada, Lebanon, Brazil, Tunisia, Albania and Cambodia. Have fun!

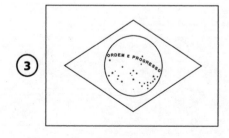

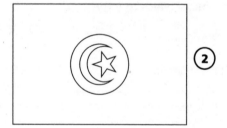

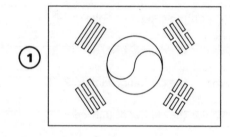

ORDEM E PROGRESSO

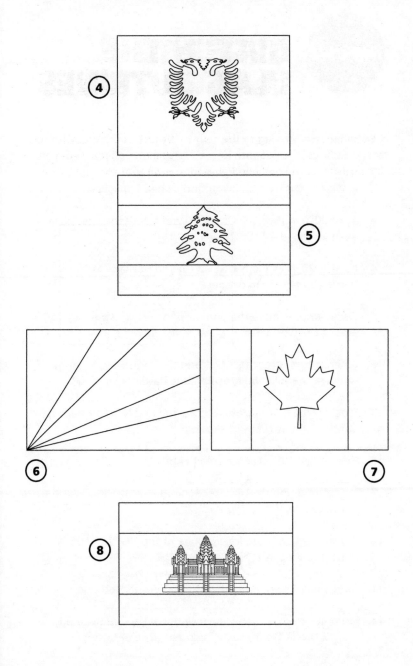

GENERAL UNESCO TRIVIA

1. What does UNESCO stand for?

2. UNESCO provides protection to sites all over the globe, but in which country would you find its headquarters?

3. As of 2020, how many UNESCO World Heritage Sites have been inscribed – 411, 821 or 1,121?

4. As of 2020, how many UNESCO World Heritage Sites are classified as being in danger?

5. Two countries share the honour of having the most UNESCO sites in the world. Can you name them both?

6. When it comes to UNESCO World Heritage Sites, what do Andorra, Angola and Mozambique have in common?

7. It may come as a surprise, but Ireland and Namibia each have only how many UNESCO sites?

8. How many UNESCO sites are in France?

9. An entire city in the UK is recognised as a UNESCO World Heritage Site. Which city is it?

10. Which German cathedral was one of the first 12 UNESCO sites to be inscribed in 1978?

11. Does Sierra Leone have any UNESCO World Heritage Sites?

12. Ethiopia's Lalibela and Simien National Park were among the first 12 UNESCO sites to be inscribed. True or false?

13. Morne Trois Pitons NP is the only UNESCO site of where?

14. The removal of a UNESCO site is rare, and Dresden Elbe Valley in Germany is one of two. Do you know why it was delisted?

15. What was the second delisted UNESCO World Heritage Site?

16. Can you name Singapore's sole UNESCO site?

17. The Amalfi Coast is just one of many UNESCO World Heritage Sites in Italy. In total, how many are there – 25, 40 or 55?

18. UNESCO has declared more than 700 Biosphere Reserves to date, defined as 'learning places for sustainable development'. The island of La Gomera is one. In which archipelago would you find it?

19. Does Bhutan have any UNESCO World Heritage Sites?

20. How many UNESCO World Heritage Sites are in Georgia?

21. Which two Ecuadorian UNESCO sites were among the first 12 to be inscribed?

22. How old is UNESCO, as of 2020?

23. How many UNESCO World Heritage Sites are in Japan?

24. Does Belize have any UNESCO World Heritage Sites?

25. Most UNESCO sites are classified as either cultural or natural, but a few are considered mixed. Is Ibiza one of them?

26. Which of the following is not inscribed on the UNESCO list of Intangible Cultural Heritage: Beer Culture in Belgium; Chinese Shadow Puppetry; Reggae, Jamaica or Morris Dancing, UK?

CULTURAL UNESCO WONDERS

1. As of 2020, how many cultural UNESCO World Heritage Sites are there – fewer or more than 800?

2. In which country are the UNESCO-listed Champagne Hillsides, Houses and Cellars?

3. Why is Lumbini, Nepal UNESCO-listed?

4. Which three cities of greater Kyoto make up the Historic Monuments of Ancient Kyoto UNESCO site?

5. In which country would you find the city of Potosí, a cultural UNESCO World Heritage Site?

6. Of the 100-plus temples at Sambor Prei Kuk in Cambodia, 10 are a shape unique in South-East Asia – what's the shape?

7. On which coast of Colombia would you find the UNESCO-inscribed Port of Cartagena: Pacific or Caribbean?

8. In which modern-day country is the UNESCO-listed archaeological site of Troy?

9. Which South African island is inscribed as a cultural site?

10. The Churches of Chiloé in Chile are most notable for being (partly) made of which material?

11. The Historic Town of Sukhothai can be found in which South-East Asian country?

12. Is the State of Liberty a cultural UNESCO World Heritage Site?

13. Eight of Ravenna, Italy's early historic monuments are UNESCO-listed. Which religion created these monuments?

14. Which Guatemalan city, dating back to the 16th century, is listed as a cultural UNESCO site?

15. Which Maltese city was listed as a cultural World Heritage Site in 1980?

16. Which ethnic group has tended to the UNESCO-listed Rice Terraces of the Philippine Cordilleras for thousands of years?

17. The Tsodilo Hills in Botswana were inscribed for having one of the highest concentrations of… what?

18. Can you name the UNESCO-listed archaeological park in Huila, Colombia known for its megalithic sculptures?

19. The ancient ruins of Babylon in Iraq were surprisingly inscribed very recently – in which year?

20. Three of the world's botanic gardens are inscribed as cultural UNESCO sites. Two are in Europe, one in Asia. What are they?

21. In October 2020 a giant new geoglyph was discovered at the Nazca Lines, Peru. What animal does it portray?

22. Is Sydney Opera House a cultural UNESCO World Heritage Site?

23. Can you name the green-and-gold-domed cathedral that forms part of Kiev's only cultural UNESCO site?

24. In which Middle Eastern country will you find the Land of Frankincense?

NATURAL UNESCO GEMS

1. As of 2020, how many natural UNESCO World Heritage Sites are there – more or fewer than 200?

2. The wildlife-rich Okavango Delta is one of the world's most extraordinary landscapes. Where is it?

3. Which bay in Australia is inscribed for its dugongs, extensive sea grass beds and stromatolites?

4. With over 850 bird species and plenty of jaguars, it's no wonder Manú National Park is UNESCO-listed. Which country can you find it in?

5. Ha Long Bay in Vietnam is known for its breathtaking beauty, uninhabited islands and outcrops made of which stone?

6. The Ancient and Primeval Beech Forests of the Carpathians and Other Regions of Europe UNESCO Site stretches over 12 countries – name two of them.

7. In which UNESCO-listed Filipino national park would you find the Jessie Beazley Reef?

8. The Western Ghats is a mountain range older than the Himalayas and one of the world's top biodiversity hotspots. Which country is it in?

9. The Western Tien-Shan mountain range is a transboundary UNESCO site spanning three countries. Can you name one?

10. Which three countries flank the Wadden Sea UNESCO Natural World Heritage Site?

11. Tsingy de Bemaraha's limestone towers are among Madagascar's great sights.... but what does tsingy mean?

12. On which UNESCO-listed island would you find South Korea's tallest mountain, Hallasan?

13. In which country would you find Durmitor National Park?

14. Sri Lanka's two natural UNESCO sites are called… what?

15. The UK's Jurassic Coast is a natural UNESCO site. Through which two counties does the UNESCO-protected part of the coast stretch?

16. What is the UNESCO-listed Vredefort Dome in South Africa?

17. In which country would you find La Siberia Biosphere Reserve? Hint: It's not Russia.

18. To the nearest hundred, how many types of coral live in the UNESCO-listed Great Barrier Reef?

19. What is the Laurisilva of Madeira?

20. Darien National Park in Panama is contiguous with Los Katios, another natural UNESCO site in which country?

21. In which country would you find Cao Bang UNESCO Global Geopark?

22. Which UNESCO-inscribed volcano is the most active in Europe (and possibly the world) and where is it?

23. Venezuela's UNESCO-listed Canaima National Park lies on the border with which two countries?

24. Which countries share the Julian Alps Biosphere Reserve?

NATURAL WONDERS

The world's natural beauty (and, sometimes, immense power) inspires so many of us to travel.

How often have you journeyed far just to wander through forest in a beautiful national park, gawp at a spectacular waterfall or hike to the peak of a craggy mountain?

Even if you're yet to visit many of the world's great wonders, you'll have seen and admired them in nature documentaries and in the pages of your favourite travel magazine.

Test yourself on these breathtaking natural highlights – from the Amazon Rainforest and the Atacama Desert to the islands of the Indian Ocean and the deep blue waters of the Pacific…

RARE RAINFORESTS

1. According to NASA, what are the two types of rainforest?

2. Can you name the eight countries (and one territory) that the Amazon Rainforest covers?

3. We all know the Amazon is the world's largest rainforest, but can you name the second largest?

4. An animal with a stripey backside found in the Congo is sometimes called the Forest Giraffe. What's its real name?

5. One of the best-loved rainforest-dwelling creatures is the sloth. What is the maximum number of toes a sloth can have?

6. The Monteverde Cloud Forest Reserve is found where?

7. In which Australian state is the Daintree Rainforest?

8. The Danum Valley is one of the world's most complex ecosystems. In which country would you find it?

9. In which continent's rainforest would you find anacondas, ocelots and howler monkeys?

10. Alaska is home to the world's largest remaining temperate rainforest. What is its name?

11. Which country beginning with P is home to the indigenous forest-living Emberá people?

12. In which densely forested South American country would you find the lowland tropical forest Iwokrama?

BREATHTAKING FORESTS

1. Which country has the highest percentage of forest cover?

2. Three countries have exactly zero per cent forest cover. Can you name all three?

3. Boreal forests, which make up roughly a third of all forest cover, are commonly known by which Russian word?

4. In which country would you find the Great Bear Rainforest, home to rare 'spirit' bears?

5. The Japanese practice of *shinrin-yoku* has become known as what in the western world?

6. In which English county is the New Forest?

7. What type of forest is the UNESCO World Heritage-listed Sundarbans in Asia?

8. In which country would you find the incredibly green, much-Instagrammed Sagano Bamboo Forest?

9. One of the world's most famous forests is Germany's Black Forest. What type of sweet food is it known for?

10. Pine, beech, American and Asian yellow-throated are all types of what furry forest critter?

11. In which US state would you find Sequoia National Forest?

12. Where in Europe would you find the curved trees of the Crooked Forest?

FLOWER POWER

1. What is the official flower of the Azores?

2. Which African country is home to the continent's only indigenous rose species: *Rosa abyssinica*?

3. From September to November each year, Pretoria, South Africa, turns purple with which flowering tree?

4. Which French region is world-renowned for its awe-inspiring lavender fields?

5. In which USA location is the National Cherry Blossom Festival held each March/April?

6. In which Latin American city and country does the annual Feria de las Flores (Festival of the Flowers) take place?

7. Can you name the national flower of India?

8. Does fluffy, white Arctic cotton grass actually grow in the Arctic Circle?

9. What is the national flower of Scotland?

10. In which Dutch town would you find the Keukenhof garden, featuring over seven million tulips?

11. Antelope Valley's poppy reserve is ablaze with orange and red flowers. What type of poppies are protected there?

12. Which pretty pink and purple flowers famously grow by New Zealand's Lake Tekapo?

Wanderlust

PICTURE QUIZ SECTION A

UNUSUAL ANIMALS

These 12 creatures are weird, wonderful and some are hard to spot. They can be found in very different parts of the world. Can you name them all? Good luck!

1

2

3

PICTURE QUIZ SECTION A

ENDANGERED SPECIES

Sadly, each of these endangered animals are growing increasingly rare. All the more reason to admire and protect them. See if you can identify each specific species...

Wanderlust

PICTURE QUIZ SECTION A
AFRICAN ANIMALS

Any safari lover will know the Big Five – but do you know all of these African animals? Time to find out!

PICTURE QUIZ SECTION A

UNUSUAL CATS

Can you correctly match the names and photographs of these eight unusual cats, found all around the world? Choose from: Caracal, oncilla, ocelot, margay, flat-headed cat, Pallas's cat, jaguarundi and sand cat. Meow!

BEARS OF THE WORLD

Can you match up these beary cool photos with the correct bear species? Choose from: American black bear, Asiatic black bear, brown bear, giant panda, polar bear, sun bear, Andean (spectacled) bear and sloth bear. Grr!

PICTURE QUIZ SECTION A
RARE
BIRDS

Birdwatching travellers would revel in a sighting of one of these rare, endangered birds. Can you match the names to the photographs? Choose from: Great Indian bustard, Galapagos penguin, kakapo, black-tailed godwit, California condor, blue-throated macaw, red-crowned crane and bald eagle.

They may not be as rare, but they are exuberantly colourful!
Can you name each of these rainbow birds, including macaws,
quetzals, toucans and motmots, among others? Three or more
would be a very impressive score. Good luck…

FAMOUS ANIMALS

All animals are special, but a few have truly caught the public's attention – from a 180-year-old creature in Saint Helena, to a friendly Irish dolphin. Do you recognise these famous animals, and can you remember their names? Let's find out.

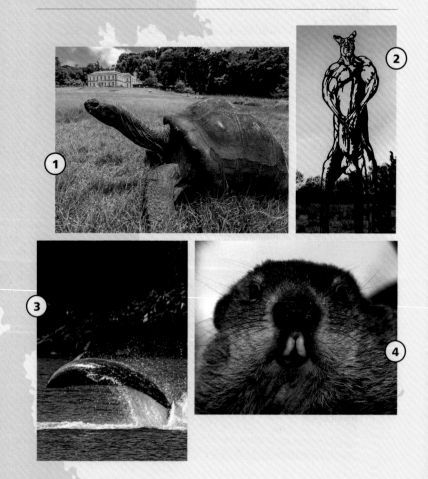

WILD WETLANDS

1. Can you name the largest freshwater wetland in the world?

2. In which country would you find the Okavango Delta?

3. What is the name of the traditional dugout canoe of the Okavango?

4. The Pantanal stretches across three countries. Brazil is one – what are the other two?

5. Which species of big cat is found throughout the Pantanal?

6. Which European wetland is famous for its white horses and black bulls?

7. What, exactly, is a Pantaneiro?

8. Which huge national park in Australia's Northern Territory is famous for its saltwater and freshwater crocodiles?

9. In which country would you find the Bangweulu Swamps, home to the black lechwe?

10. The Danube River flows through many countries, but in which country would you find its delta?

11. India's Keoladeo National Park is world famous for what type of wildlife?

12. The Sundarbans is the world's largest delta. Which three rivers flow into it?

NATIONAL PARKS

1. What and where is the world's biggest national park?

2. India's Gir Forest National Park is famous for which animal?

3. In which country would you find the distinctive orange-striped sandstone mountains of Zhangye National Geopark?

4. With soaring mountains and bright blue glaciers, in which country would you find the Torres del Paine National Park?

5. Costa Rica's Tortuguero National Park is packed with wildlife, but what exactly does the name 'Tortuguero' mean?

6. Croatia has eight breathtaking national parks. What is Plitvice, arguaby the most famous, known for?

7. What is the UK's largest national park?

8. Sri Lanka's most-visited national park is a renowned safari spot for leopard lovers. What's its name?

9. Iceland has three very famous national parks: Thingvellir, Vatnajökull and...?

10. In which country would you find the Ben Lomond National Park?

11. Guadeloupe, Réunion and Guiana Amazonian national parks are within overseas territories of which European country?

12. In which country would you find the Valley of Flowers National Park?

AFRICA PARKS

1. Can you name the largest national park in South Africa?

2. In which African country would you find the zebra-packed Etosha National Park?

3. The Great Migration of wildebeest traverses two African protected areas. Can you name them both?

4. In which countries are the two parks?

5. Which animal is South Africa's Addo National Park best known for?

6. Loango National Park is famous for its 'surfing hippos' among other wildlife. Which country is it in?

7. In which South African national park would you find the southernmost tip of Africa?

8. Bwindi Impenetrable Forest NP and the Virunga Mountains are famous for which iconic primate?

9. Which is Africa's oldest national park?

10. Madagascar's Andasibe-Mantadia National Park is the best place to see the largest of the lemur species. What's its name?

11. What natural wonder gives the Ngorongoro Conservation Area its name?

12. Zambia's South Luangwa National Park is one of the best places in the world to see which spotted feline?

USA PARKS

1. How many national parks are there in the USA – 42, 52 or 62?

2. Which national park was the first designated in the USA?

3. Which national park is the largest in the USA?

4. Can you name at least two of Utah's stunning 'Mighty Five' national parks?

5. In which national park would you find the largest hot spring in the United States, the Grand Prismatic Spring?

6. Great Smoky Mountains National Park lies on the border of which two states?

7. In which national park would you find the dizzying granite peak of El Capitan?

8. The common name for the *Yucca brevifolia* is also the name of a US national park (and U2 album). Name that tree!

9. With rugged mountains and spectacular lakes, in which state would you find Glacier National Park?

10. Acadia National Park in Maine is home to a mountain which shares the name of a classic American car. Name that mountain!

11. Which national park is home to North America's tallest peak?

12. In which state would you find the Carlsbad Caverns?

MIGHTY MOUNTAINS

1. We all know Kilimanjaro is Africa's highest mountain.
   But which is the second highest?

2. Mount Wycheproof is often touted as the world's smallest
   mountain. Where would you find it?

3. Which lofty Asian peak is named after a Victorian surveyor of
   India?

4. If you were measuring from the centre of the earth, which
   mountain is the world's highest and where is it?

5. In which country will you find Mount Damavand?

6. Which two countries are home to the Matterhorn?

7. International bodies recognise mountains over 8,000m tall
   as 'eight-thousanders'. How many are there – 11 or 14?

8. On which island would you find the highest mountain
   in Japan, Mount Fuji?

9. What is Nepal's sacred Machapuchare popularly known as?

10. According to Guinness World Records, where would you find
    the world's oldest mountain range?

11. Michael Palin said that "*Wanderlust* is the best travel
    magazine this side of..." which mountain in Pakistan?

12. Can you name the highest peak in China's Huangshan
    Mountain Range?

FAMOUS HILLS

1. Which Italian city is commonly said to have been built on seven hills?

2. In which city would you find the hill called Arthur's Seat?

3. Bohol province in the Philippines is known for its extraordinary cone-shaped hills. What sweet treat are they named for?

4. The chalk figure carved into the side of Uffington Hill in Oxfordshire, England represents what animal?

5. In which English county would you find the grassy, 517m-high hill Mam Tor?

6. Maungakiekie, a volcanic peak in Auckland, New Zealand, is more famously known as what hill?

7. County Meath in Ireland is home to a famous hill with a woman's name. Can you name that hill?

8. What sits atop the Penshaw Hill in north-east England?

9. The Cypress Hills (a mix of forest, wetland and grassland) are found in which country, beginning with a 'C'?

10. On which Scottish island would you find the jagged hill named the Old Man of Storr?

11. Which Indian hill station served as the summer capital of the Raj?

12. In which Asian country would you find the Vetal Tekdi hill?

FIERY VOLCANOES

1. Mauna Loa is the world's largest volcano. Where is it?

2. Which country has the most volcanoes – both active and dormant – in the world?

3. What name is given to the series of countries around the Pacific noted for volcanic activity?

4. The 'Avenue of Volcanoes', along which lies Cotopaxi, is in which country?

5. The active Arenal Volcano is found where?

6. Tenerife is home to the third-largest volcanic structure in the world. What's it called?

7. Vesuvius is one of the world's best-known volcanoes. In which Italian region would you find it?

8. In which country would you find Mount Tambora?

9. What is the locals' nickname for Mexico's most famous volcano, Popocatépetl?

10. Which Icelandic volcano erupted in 2010, emitting vast ash clouds that caused huge disruption to international air travel?

11. What is the term for a large crater, formed when a volcano's empty magma chamber collapses?

12. Where would you find the dormant Mount Ararat?

DRY DESERTS

1. A desert has to be covered in sand. True or false?

2. What is the world's biggest desert (by area)?

3. According to NASA, which desert is the driest in the world and in which country would you find it?

4. Known for its massive chalk rock formations, where would you find the White Desert?

5. North America has four major deserts, including Mojave, Chihuahuan and Sonoran. Can you remember the fourth?

6. The Mojave Desert spans which four US states?

7. Which British explorer wrote *Arabian Sands* about his time crossing the Empty Quarter?

8. Would you find the huge Kalahari Desert in northern or southern Africa?

9. The Gobi Desert spreads across two East Asian countries. Which are they?

10. Antarctica is technically classed as a desert. True or false?

11. Which type of camel would you find in the deserts of Central Asia? And how many humps does it have?

12. In which country and province would you find Tabernas, often called 'the only desert in mainland Europe'?

HOT SPRINGS

1. In which country is Geysir, after which other spouting hot springs are named?

2. Can you name the world's largest hot spring?

3. In which Caribbean country would you find the Boiling Lake?

4. What is the Japanese name for a natural hot spring, many of which are used for bathing?

5. In which city and country will you find the famous Art Nouveau Gellert thermal baths?

6. Diamond Geyser in Orakei Korako, New Zealand regularly erupts. How high can the water shoot up?

7. With an average year-round temperature around 38°C/100°F, what is the name of the famous Geothermal Spa in south-west Iceland?

8. The USA's Steamboat Geyser erupts often. In which national park could you witness this natural spectacle?

9. In which US state would you find the appropriately named town of Hot Springs?

10. Where are the otherworldly Pamukkale Thermal Pools?

11. In which English city can you visit naturally heated baths constructed by the Romans in AD 70?

12. Where in the world would you find the Banjar Hot Springs?

CURIOUS CAVES

1. What is the world's largest (natural) cave and where is it?

2. What is the name of the world's longest known cave system?

3. Which Italian city is commonly referred to as the 'cave city'?

4. Which region in Turkey is famous for its cave churches and 'fairy chimney' rock formations?

5. Known for its natural acoustics, on which Scottish island is the aesthetically pleasing Fingal's Cave?

6. The Waitomo Caves in New Zealand can be explored by boat, raft or tube. But what are they famous for?

7. Predjama Castle is a Renaissance castle built inside the mouth of a cave. In which country is it found?

8. Mexico's Yucatán Peninsula is home to countless jaw-dropping cenotes, but what exactly is a cenote?

9. In which country would you find the spectacular Smoo Cave?

10. In which country would you find the distinctive Marble Caves on General Carrera Lake?

11. A major attraction in Thailand's Prachuap Khiri Khan Province is a temple built inside which cave?

12. In which country would you hike, swim and wade into Actun Tunichil Muknal caves to see Mayan remains?

OUT-OF-THIS-WORLD OCEANS

1. Which ocean is the largest and deepest?

2. Which ocean is the smallest and most shallow?

3. According to NASA, which of the oceans is the saltiest?

4. Madagascar, Mauritius and Comoros are all islands situated in which ocean?

5. Which museum in Nova Scotia houses the largest collection of artefacts from the *Titanic*, which sank in the Atlantic Ocean?

6. Can you name the deepest known point in the Pacific Ocean?

7. In which ocean would you find the world's largest coral reef system, The Great Barrier Reef?

8. The Atlantic Ocean laps many countries. Are Spain, Portugal and Saint Lucia among them?

9. The Bermuda Triangle is a mysterious region in which ocean?

10. Do you know which chilly ocean the crocodile icefish, also known as the white-blooded fish, resides in?

11. How much of the world's surface is covered by ocean: around 30, 50 or 70 per cent?

12. In which three oceans would you find the Olive Ridley sea turtle?

INCREDIBLE ISLANDS

1. Which island is the biggest in the world, with an area of 2,130,800 sq km?

2. The world's smallest island nation is in the Pacific Ocean. What's it called?

3. Can you name the biggest Caribbean island?

4. Which is the remotest island on the planet, according to Guinness World Records?

5. How many Greek islands are there, to the nearest thousand?

6. Both Ascension and Inaccessible islands belong to which UK overseas territory?

7. The nation of Malta consists of three islands. Name all three.

8. The Dragon's Blood Tree is so-called because of the red sap it produces. Which island is it native to?

9. What is the modern Polynesian name for Easter Island?

10. In which country is the island of Komodo, home to its eponymous 'dragon', a huge carnivorous reptile?

11. In which region and country would you find 'Rabbit Island'?

12. In which archipelago would you find Isabela Island, which is packed with wildlife?

SEAS OF THE WORLD

1. The world's largest inland body of water is called a sea. Can you name it?

2. The Red Sea is an extension of which ocean?

3. Sunny Antigua, Montserrat, Saint Martin and Nevis are all islands in which sea?

4. Which two countries have shores on the Sea of Okhotsk?

5. The deep sea creature 'blob sculpin' can be found in which ocean?

6. Pag, Mljet, Kolocep and Lopud are all stunning islands located in which sea?

7. In which specific sea would you most commonly find the gilt-head bream?

8. Where is the Ross Sea?

9. Which sea lies between the Bay of Bengal and southern Myanmar?

10. Between which three countries would you find the Yellow Sea?

11. Where in the world is the Sea of Marmara?

12. Which sea does the Strait of Gibraltar connect the Atlantic Ocean to?

PRETTY PENINSULAS

1. The word 'peninsula' is derived from two Latin words, 'paene' and 'insula'. What do those words mean?

2. How does a peninsula differ from an isthmus?

3. Which peninsula is the world's longest?

4. Which seven countries lie on the Arabian peninsula?

5. Which Irish peninsula is home to Fungie the dolphin and the location where the Jedi temple in *Star Wars: The Last Jedi* was filmed?

6. Aarhus, Billund and Aalborg are three Danish cities on which peninsula?

7. Is the entire US state of Alaska a peninsula?

8. In 1956, this Welsh peninsula rightly became the first Area of Outstanding Natural Beauty in the UK. Name that peninsula!

9. Mainland England's most southerly point is on a peninsula named after a reptile. Can you name (and locate) it?

10. In which region and country would you find the beautiful Yorke Peninsula with its 700km of coastline?

11. The Nicoya Peninsula is known for its surfing, turtles and yoga. Which Latin American country is it found in?

12. Known for its dramatic landscapes, which breathtaking peninsula in western Iceland is often called 'Iceland in Miniature'?

WONDERFUL WATERFALLS

1. Which waterfall is the tallest in the world at 979m high, and where is it?

2. The Denmark Strait cataract is the largest underwater waterfall in the world. In which ocean is it found?

3. Where would you find Kaieteur Falls, the world's largest single-drop waterfall by volume of water?

4. Iguazu Falls (and the national park of the same name) cascade between which two countries?

5. Niagara Falls, between the USA and Canada, comprise how many drops?

6. Situated on the south coast of Iceland, what do most visitors do at the famous Seljalandsfoss?

7. Boasting three drops, in which country would you find the ethereal Ban Gioc Falls?

8. On which southern African river would you find Victoria Falls?

9. Why is Venta Rapid in Latvia noteworthy?

10. In which English county would you find High Force waterfall?

11. On which Hawaiian island would you find Manoa Falls, Lulumahu Falls and the unusual Upside Down Waterfall?

12. Where in the world would you find the Blue Nile Falls?

RAUCOUS RIVERS

1. What is the world's longest river?

2. And what is the world's widest river?

3. Where would you find the Irrawaddy River?

4. The third largest river in the world is 6,300km long. Can you name (and locate) that river?

5. The Tigris River runs through which three countries?

6. Australia's longest river shares a name with a famous tennis player. Can you name that player?

7. How many European countries does the Danube run through – 8, 10 or 12?

8. Exactly 27 rivers flow into Lake Titicaca, but only one flows out from it. Can you name that river?

9. On which famous river can you cruise on a traditional *felucca* or *dahabiya* as well as more modern craft?

10. Do you know the name of the UK's longest river?

11. In 2017, a river in New Zealand became the first to be granted the same legal rights as a human being. What is its name?

12. Bahrain, Malta and Vatican City all have rivers. True or false?

LOVELY LAKES

1. How many lakes are there in the UK's Lake District – 12 or 16?

2. Speaking of the Lake District, do you know which county this beautiful region is situated in?

3. Where in the world would you find Lake Sevan?

4. What's the official name of the neon-green lake in New Zealand dubbed the 'Devil's Bath'?

5. What type of lake is the Dead Sea: salt or freshwater? (Yep, it's a lake...)

6. In which South American lake are the 'floating' Uros Islands?

7. The freshwater lake Tonlé Sap is close to the largest religious monument in the world. In which country would you find it?

8. What colour is Lake Hillier, located in Western Australia? (Hint: it's not blue...)

9. Can you name at least two of North America's five interconnected Great Lakes?

10. Which lake in Africa has the largest surface area?

11. Loch Ness, home of the legendary monster, is the largest Scottish loch by volume. Which is the deepest?

12. Set in a massive volcanic crater, in which Central American country would you find Lake Atitlán?

MANMADE MARVELS

These quizzes shift focus from the world's natural wonders to those created by people.

Whether it's the Seven Wonders (both ancient and new), fascinating civilisations dating back thousands of years, modern cities bursting with art and architecture or eerie abandoned places that have an unusual 'extreme tourism' appeal, you certainly won't be short on questions to answer.

And if you think you know all there is to know about the planet's grandest palaces, castles, temples and mosques, then you're in for a real treat…

PERFECT PALACES

1. Where in the world would you find Potala Palace?

2. At what time can you typically see the Changing of the Guard ceremony outside Buckingham Palace?

3. In which Asian city and country would you find the magnificent Gyeongbokgung Palace?

4. Can you name the iconic mint-green palace in St Petersburg that now houses the Hermitage Museum?

5. The popular Vienna attraction, Schönbrunn Palace, used to serve as the summer residence for which royal dynasty?

6. In which Portuguese city's hills would you find the yellow and fuchsia castle known as the National Palace of Pena?

7. In which Indian state would you find the majestic Amber Fort, sometimes known as Amber Palace?

8. Which breathtaking palace complex in Beijing, built by the Qing dynasty, is the largest royal garden complex in China?

9. In which palace do the Danish Royal Family live?

10. How many rooms has the Palace of Versailles - 1,100 or 2,300?

11. In which European city and country would you find the Renaissance-style Pitti Palace?

12. Can you name the palace residence of the Princely Family of Liechtenstein?

DRAMATIC CASTLES

1. The fairytale Neuschwanstein Castle is instantly recognisable, but in which region and country is it found ?

2. Leeds Castle in the United Kingdom isn't located in the city of Leeds. Where is it?

3. Which is the oldest and largest inhabited castle in the world?

4. Wales is famous for its impressive castles. Which is the biggest (also the name of a hard, crumbly cheese)?

5. In which country would you find Orava Castle?

6. The USA isn't known for its castles, but in which state would you find the pretty, 20th century-Hearst Castle?

7. In which Scottish county is Queen Elizabeth II's beloved holiday home, Balmoral Castle?

8. The medieval Fort Santa Cruz stands tall in Oran. Which North African country does it belong to?

9. The ruins of which Japanese castle are often referred to as 'Japan's Machu Picchu'?

10. Which (real) Transylvanian castle is commonly known as Dracula's Castle?

11. Where would you find the Castillo de San Felipe de Barajas?

12. In which African country would you find the European-style Duwisib Castle, built by a German captain?

FASCINATING MUSEUMS

1. Which museum, due to open in late 2020, claims to be the largest archaeological museum in the world?

2. What and where is the oldest museum in Peru?

3. In which country would you find the colourful Pysanka Easter Egg Museum?

4. Can you name the museum which sits 2,275m above sea level atop Mount Kronplatz in Italy?

5. In which country would you find the unique Museum of Broken Relationships?

6. China's ancient city of Xi'an marked the end of the Silk Road. Now it is more famous for the nearby museum housing what?

7. You can find museums dedicated to samurai, Studio Ghibli, sand sculptures and instant ramen in Japan. True or false?

8. In which century did the UK's National History Museum open?

9. Which country in the Caucasus is home to a dedicated carpet museum (complete with a carpet-shaped roof)?

10. In which town would you find the Dutch Cheese Museum?

11. Which famous British explorer is buried in the cemetery close to South Georgia Museum in Grytviken?

12. In which European country would you find the Frietmuseum, which is dedicated to the history of potatoes and fries?

ART GALLERIES

1. Can you name the world's largest art museum?

2. In which year did New York's MoMA first open its doors?

3. Where in the Netherlands can you see Van Gogh's *Sunflowers*, *Almond Blossom* and *Self-Portrait with Grey Felt Hat*?

4. The eclectic Owl House in Nieu Bethesda, South Africa was created by which artist?

5. Where would you find Frida Kahlo's 1939 work *The Two Fridas* on display?

6. Where would you find the four completed Guggenheim modern art museums?

7. The Mauritshuis in The Hague houses which famous painting: *The Kiss*, *Mona Lisa* or *Girl with a Pearl Earring*?

8. Where would you find the 1930s reconstruction of Babylon's spectacular Ishtar Gate?

9. Uruguay's Espacio de Arte Contemporáneo is an art space located inside a converted… what?

10. Which Japanese art collective is behind the immersive, light-based *Borderless World* and *Forest of Lamps* exhibits?

11. Where is Leonard Da Vinci's *The Last Supper* displayed?

12. The extraordinary underwater sculptures of MUSA are close to which Mexican city?

FAMOUS CITIES

1. Two Nicaraguan cities share their names with cities in Spain. Can you name them?

2. Which German city is home to the world's narrowest street?

3. Shanghai is famous for, among other things, its theme parks. In 2020, one opened about which blue cartoon characters?

4. Can you name all five of New York City's boroughs?

5. The residents of Newcastle-upon-Tyne, northern England are given which affectionate collective nickname?

6. Ushuaia, Argentina is often considered the world's southernmost city, but in 2019 a Chilean town changed its status in order to nab the title. Which town (now city) is it?

7. Which river bisects the Czech capital city, Prague?

8. What's the name of Malta's walled city, less than a square kilometre in size, and sometimes known as the 'silent city'?

9. The name of Kenya's capital, Nairobi, has a distinct aquatic meaning taken from a Maasai phrase. What does it mean?

10. In which French region would you find the city of Paris?

11. London, Windsor and Surrey are all places in the UK and cities in Canada. Is this statement correct?

12. Japan's second-biggest city (by population) may come as a surprise. Do you know what it is?

UNUSUAL TOWNS

1. Chichicastenango and its vibrant outdoor market can be found in which Central American county?

2. What is the name given to the distinctive whitewashed, conical-roofed stone buildings found in Alberobello, Puglia?

3. Roswell, New Mexico is best known for its eerie extraterrestrial connections. In which year did its famous UFO incident reputedly occur?

4. In which two South American countries would you find towns named New (Nieuw) Amsterdam?

5. Which UK town shot to fame after the Prime Minister's chief advisor was spotted visiting during the first COVID lockdown?

6. Which two lakes sit either side of Interlaken, Switzerland?

7. In which Serbian town does the joyous trumpet festival take place each August, attracting 600,000 visitors?

8. The Moroccan town of Chefchaouen is famous for being painted which colour?

9. In which African country is the adobe town of Djenné?

10. What are the Chinese towns Qiandeng, Tongli and Zhouzhuang all examples of?

11. Near which Sri Lankan town would you find Sigiriya Fortress?

12. Which New Zealand town's name translates to 'second lake'?

EUROPEAN OLD TOWNS

1. In which city would you find Gamla Stan, the orange-hued, 17th century Old Town?

2. In which Polish city will you find Rynek Starego Miasta?

3. One of Europe's best Old Towns can be found in Bruges, but how old is the Belfry of Bruges – 500, 600 or 800 years?

4. Which Baltic capital's UNESCO-listed Old Town is dominated by hilltop Toompea Castle?

5. The Old Town of Norway's second-largest city also has World Heritage status. Can you name it?

6. Which UNESCO-listed Granada neighbourhood allows you to discover Medieval Moorish history?

7. Lovrijenac Tower is found in which Croatian Old Town?

8. The old walled town of Montreuil-sur-Mer inspired which 19th-century book which went on to be a successful musical?

9. In which Austrian Old Town would you find the birthplace of Wolfgang Amadeus Mozart?

10. Which walled French city is home to Château Comtal?

11. Which market square in Edinburgh's Old Town sold cattle in the 14th century?

12. Which historic Spanish city is set either side of the spectacular El Tajo gorge?

FAMOUS VILLAGES

1. Giethoorn in the Netherlands is (almost) completely free of which popular form of transportation?

2. Which Austrian village was famously replicated in China?

3. Is the UK village of Mousehole in Devon, Cornwall or Dorset?

4. Can you name the largest of the five UNESCO-protected Cinque Terre villages (by area)?

5. In which country would you find the ghost village of Villa Epecuén?

6. Which European country is home to Popeye Village, a 1980s film set that became a popular tourist attraction?

7. Designer William Morris called which Cotswolds settlement the 'most beautiful village in England'?

8. In which country would you find the village of Sidi Bou Said?

9. The village of Hogsback inspired JRR Tolkein's Middle Earth in *The Hobbit*. Which country is it in?

10. On which Greek island would you find the village of Oia?

11. Which Scottish village would you start in if you were looking to traverse the UK from north to south, to Land's End, Cornwall?

12. Vung Vieng is Vietnam is one of the few examples of what type of village? Whereabouts is it?

STATUES & MONUMENTS

1. Which statue, completed in 2018, is the world's tallest?

2. In which UK town would you find *The Scallop*, a steel statue inspired by composer Benjamin Britten?

3. Where in the world would you find the bronze Christ of the Abyss statue?

4. Which country gave The Statue of Liberty to the USA?

5. Atop Buzludzha Peak in Bulgaria is a UFO-shaped monument. But is it actually space-related?

6. In which country would you find the African Renaissance Monument?

7. Who features on the huge Equestrian Statue near Ulaanbaatar in Mongolia?

8. In which year was work complete on the instantly-recognisable Leshan Giant Buddha in China – AD 803, 1103 or 1503?

9. In which European city and country would you find the Motherland Monument, also called Rodina Mat?

10. What is the modern Polynesian name of Easter Island, home to the famous Moai head statues?

11. In which city would you find the Manneken Pis statue?

12. Do you know what's depicted in De Vaartkapoen, a comedic statue in Belgium?

INCREDIBLE ARCHITECTURE

1. Who had the Taj Mahal in India built in memory of his wife?

2. Antoni Gaudí spent his life creating unusual, colourful buildings, mostly in which city?

3. The Leaning Tower of Pisa leans by just under.... 4, 7 or 9 degrees?

4. A fine example of pre-Saharan architecture is the Ksar (citadel) of Aït-Ben-Haddou. Where in Morocco is it?

5. The Sistine Chapel in the Apostolic Palace of the Vatican epitomises which period of art and architecture?

6. Can you name the architect who built New York City's iconic Chrysler Building?

7. How did Danish architect Jørn Utzon famously come to design the Sydney Opera House in 1957?

8. What is the tallest building in the world, at 828m high?

9. In which century was Egypt's Great Pyramid of Khufu built?

10. Where would you find the collection of Bauhaus houses known as the White City?

11. Where would you find the stylish Château Frontenac, often called the 'world's most photographed hotel'?

12. Which French structure is nicknamed 'La Dame de Fer'?

THE SEVEN WONDERS

1. In which year did the results of a public vote reveal the New Seven Wonders of the World – 1997 or 2007?

2. How many of the Ancient Seven Wonders of the World remain standing today?

3. Though it no longer stands, you can still visit the site of the Pharos lighthouse today – where?

4. Which modern day country would the Temple of Artemis stand in now?

5. In which Brazilian city would you find the Christ the Redeemer statue, one of the New Seven Wonders?

6. The Maya city of Chichén Itzá is in which Mexican state?

7. An unsurprising addition to the list: the Great Wall of China. Do you know long it is (in km)? For an extra point, can it be seen from space with the naked eye?

8. What is the Taj Mahal's actual purpose?

9. The Christ the Redeemer statue is made of which materials?

10. What is the Flavian Amphitheatre better known as?

11. Can you name the large central pyramid at the Mayan site of Chichén Itzá?

12. The majority of visitors to Petra enter through the atmospheric narrow, twisting passage known as 'The...'?

ABANDONED PLACES

1. Which US ghost town has had a coal mine burning beneath it since 1962?

2. Can you name the Ukrainian ghost city abandoned following the 1986 Chernobyl nuclear disaster?

3. Great Zimbabwe is now a ruin. What was it in its heyday?

4. What is the name of the abandoned lighthouse in Denmark which is disappearing into shifting sand?

5. The spooky ghost town of Kolmanskop in Namibia lies in which desert?

6. What happened to Villa Epecuén in 1985, turning it into Argentina's most famous ghost town?

7. Where is the abandoned whaling station of Grytviken?

8. What happened in abandoned Wittenoom, Australia, for it be declared as a 'contaminated site'?

9. Shengshan Island, China was once home to a fishing village. Now it's abandoned and covered in vines. What's it called?

10. Which Italian region is home to the abandoned town of Craco?

11. This forgotten gold miner's route in New Zealand has since become a popular cycling trail. Can you name the road?

12. Speaking of gold mining, Bodie is an abandoned mining town in which US state?

ANCIENT CIVILISATIONS

1. The archaeological site Caracol in Belize comprises ruins from which ancient civilisation?

2. Colombia's lost city of Teyuna (Ciudad Perdida) was built by which ancient people?

3. The 16th-century archaeological site Nan Madol is located in which island country?

4. In which century is it believed that the Inca built Machu Picchu?

5. Where is the world's most famous ancient Acropolis?

6. Which ancient civilisation built the Rose Red City of Petra?

7. In which Central American country would you find the Maya site El Mirador?

8. Mesa Verde National Park in Colorado protects the heritage of which Native American people?

9. In which century did the Romans build the Colosseum?

10. In which country would you find the archaeological remains of Persepolis, the jewel of the Achaemenid Empire?

11. The Historic City of Ayutthaya was, many centuries ago, also the capital of which Asian country?

12. In which modern city can you find the remains of the ancient Phoenician city of Carthage?

PICTURE QUIZ SECTION B

ANCIENT SITES

Can you identify these ruins, ancient civilisations and archaeological points of interest from just one picture? We're after the name of the site. Bonus points if you know which country it's in, too. Give it your best shot!

1

2

3

PICTURE QUIZ SECTION B
GUESS THE UNESCO SITE

Having already tested your UNESCO trivia, let's see how well you can identify some of the world's most popular UNESCO World Heritage Sites – using just one photograph. We're after the site's name (not necessarily its 'official' UNESCO name) and bonus points for the country it's in.

WHERE WAS THIS TAKEN?

Here we have eight snaps for eight destinations loved by travellers. Your task? Try to determine which country each photograph was taken. Enjoy!

1

2

3

4

MATCH THE STREET SIGNS

In any city or town on our travels, we have to navigate a host of street (and road) signs. Can you match these street signs to their country of origin? Choose from: Spain, England, Russia, Colombia, Austria, Japan, New Zealand and France.

1

2

3

·NO NAME · STREET

(4)

PLAZA DE LA TRINIDAD

(5)

CAUTION NEXT 5 km

(6)

8ᵉ ARRᵀ

AVENUE DES CHAMPS ÉLYSÉES

(7)

(8)

1547   1616

CALLE DE CERVANTES

PICTURE QUIZ SECTION B
UNUSUAL STATUES

Some of these may have popped up on your travels. Even if not, can you match the country to the statue – Chile, Colombia, Czech Republic, India, Kyrgyzstan, Norway, Ukraine, USA?

5

6

7

8

PICTURE QUIZ SECTION B

COLOURFUL BUILDINGS

These neon, rainbow and brightly-coloured buildings are world-famous. Do you know which country you can find each one in? See if you can correctly locate them.

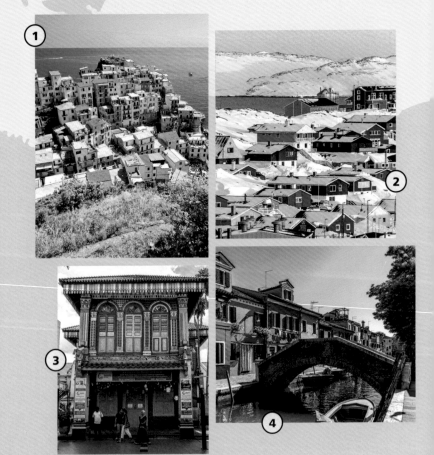

PICTURE QUIZ SECTION B
UNUSUAL FLAGS

This quiz is straightforward. Match all 12 flags to their correct country. Choose from: San Marino, Kyrgyzstan, Azerbaijan, Papua New Guinea, Dominica, Thailand, Zimbabwe, Bhutan, Serbia, Denmark, Tanzania and Portugal. Good luck!

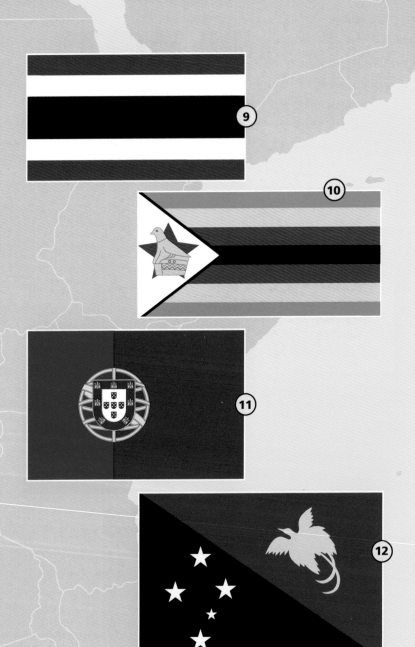

FANTASTIC FOUNTAINS

1. Which fountain was in Federico Fellini's 1960 film *La Dolce Vita*?

2. Which Las Vegas fountain is renowned for its three-minute water-and-light display?

3. Which crystal company created the grass-covered, face-shaped fountain in Wattens, Austria?

4. If it is 3pm GMT, what time would the famous Osaka Clock Fountain in Japan say?

5. In which Middle Eastern Emirate would you find an indoor fountain dramatically decorated with pearl divers?

6. In which US state did the 1500s explorer Juan Ponce de León believe the mythical Fountain of Youth could be found?

7. The Fountain of Wealth ISN'T a myth. Where in Asia is it?

8. From which bridge in South Korea does the 1,140m-long Moonlight Rainbow Fountain spray?

9. How many fountains does London's Trafalgar Square have?

10. In which European city will you find the impressive 140m-high Jet d'Eau fountain?

11. The Friendship of Nations Fountain can be found in which former Soviet city and country?

12. There are two fountains named Diana in London's parks. Where can you see them?

SACRED TEMPLES

1. This grand, domed temple on Java is the world's largest Buddhist monument. What's it called?

2. To which God is India's UNESCO-listed Konark Sun Temple devoted?

3. How big is the temple Angkor Wat and the surrounding archaeological site in Cambodia – 201 sq km or 401 sq km?

4. Which Sri Lankan city boasts the Temple of the Tooth?

5. What is the official name of the White Temple, Thailand's all-white temple-and-art-exhibit?

6. Which golden pagoda sits atop Singuttara Hill in Yangon, Myanmar (Burma)?

7. In which country would you find the Paro Taktsang temple complex built into a cliff?

8. In which century was the iconic Boudhanath stupa in Kathmandu, Nepal built – 14th, 15th or 16th?

9. Which temple in Lhasa houses the Jowo Sakyamuni, the most sacred statue in Tibet?

10. In which city will you find the Buddhist temple Kinkaku-ji?

11. In which country is the 1984 film *Indiana Jones and the Temple of Doom* mostly set?

12. In which Asian city would you find the Temple of Heaven?

MAGNIFICENT MOSQUES

1. In which country on the Arabian Peninsula would you find the world's largest mosque?

2. Where can you find the largest mosque in Central Asia?

3. What is the official name of Istanbul's famous tiled Blue Mosque?

4. In which Spanish region is the Mosque-Cathedral of Córdoba?

5. In which Uzbek city does the completely rebuilt Bibi-Khanym Mosque stand?

6. To which two religions is the Dome of the Rock most sacred?

7. How many minarets surround the modern Faisal Mosque in Islamabad, Pakistan?

8. Which mosque do you think ranked as the world's third-favourite landmark on TripAdvisor in 2018?

9. In which Moroccan city would you find the Hassan II Mosque?

10. The Great Mosque of Samarra, in Iraq, was built in which century – 7th, 9th or 11th?

11. How many domes sit atop the breathtaking Badshahi Mosque in Lahore, Pakistan?

12. When Oman's Sultan Qaboos Grand Mosque opened in Muscat in 2001 it claimed to have the world's biggest what?

CHURCHES & CATHEDRALS

1. Saint Basil's Cathedral's multi-coloured exterior is legendary, as is its notorious creator, Ivan the... who?

2. Brazilian architect Oscar Niemeyer designed which UNESCO-listed cathedral?

3. What's the name of Iceland's largest church?

4. The extraordinary Zipaquira Cathedral is found underground in a salt mine. In which country is it?

5. What is special about how Temppeliaukio Church, in Helsinki, was built?

6. Which religion is worshipped in the Cathedral of Salta, Argentina?

7. In which Serbian city would you find the rainbow-spired Name of Mary Church?

8. To the nearest thousand, how many human skeletons make up the Czech Republic's bone church, Sedlec Ossuary?

9. What is Iglesia el Rosario in El Salvador best known for?

10. Is the Sagrada Familia, Barcelona's cathedral, finished?

11. Why is England's Westminster Abbey called an abbey... when really, it's a church?

12. In which country would you find the cave chapels and monasteries of the Kadisha Valley?

PEACEFUL MONASTERIES

1. Davit Gareja and Gelati are just two of many famous monasteries found in which country?

2. In which rose-red city in Jordan will you find an impressive Nabatean tomb known as The Monastery?

3. On the banks of which UK river is Tintern Abbey?

4. Can you name the Greek rock formation on which several monasteries are built?

5. Pecherska Lavra is Kiev's most prominent monastery, but what does the name actually mean?

6. The Ostrog Monastery is in Montenegro, but which religion is practiced here?

7. Three Portuguese monasteries are UNESCO World Heritage Sites. Can you name just one?

8. In which country will you find Taktsang Monastery, aka the Tiger's Nest?

9. Where would you find the monastery Khor Virap?

10. Where in Europe would you find the bright yellow, palace-like Melk Abbey?

11. What is the name of the precipitous Irish island which was home to a monastery and features in *Star Wars*?

12. The Painted Monasteries are found in which Romanian city?

BRIDGES & VIADUCTS

1. Which California bridge appears in numerous TV shows and films, including HBO's *Big Little Lies*?

2. In which European city would you find the Charles Bridge?

3. Brazil's most famous arch bridge is named after which former president?

4. Which Scottish viaduct is famous for appearing alongside the Hogwarts Express in the *Harry Potter* films?

5. Do you know what the last remaining Inca rope bridge in the world is called?

6. In which Balkan country would you find the iconic Stari Most?

7. Can you name and locate the longest covered bridge in the world?

8. Is Venice, Italy home to the Bridge of Cries, Sighs or Whispers?

9. In which South American country would you find the unique, circle-shaped bridge Laguna Garzón?

10. Khaju and Si-o-se-pol bridges can both be seen in which Iranian city?

11. How high above the water do you think the iconic Sydney Harbour Bridge is – 104 or 134 metres?

12. Which two sides of a city does the grand Széchenyi Chain Bridge connect?

DAMS & RESERVOIRS

1. Cyclists love to ride past the Elan Valley Dams in Wales. How many are there?

2. Between which two countries would you find Kariba Dam?

3. Kariba Dam forms Lake Kariba, often called the world's largest manmade reservoir by volume. How long is it – 120, 180 or 220 km?

4. Another contender for the world's largest title, this time by surface area, is Lake Volta. Behind which dam, and where, is it contained?

5. The Hoover Dam borders which two US states?

6. Do you know which river is blocked by the Hoover Dam?

7. The temples of Abu Simbel were saved from the rising waters of which lake, and moved to its shoreline?

8. In which European country would you find Contra Dam?

9. Lake Calima is the largest manmade lake in...?

10. Gordon Dam in Australia is quite a sight. Can you remember what shape it is?

11. In which Canadian province would you find the manmade reservoir Williston Lake?

12. Europe's largest reservoir is a lovely place for a houseboat holiday. Where is it?

GREAT JOURNEYS

The following quizzes are all devoted to epic journeys, taken on foot or by ship, train or plane.

Some were undertaken hundreds of years ago by the world's most intrepid explorers, others are once-in-a-lifetime feats designed to garner a world record. Most of these adventures can still be taken today, if you're up for the challenge.

Walk the planet's most punishing, yet rewarding, hiking trails, or board one of the world's best train journeys. From the emptiest parts of Antarctica to the rainforest paradise of Borneo, there's still plenty left to be discovered.

For now, let's see how much you already know...

INTREPID EXPLORERS

1. Which explorer is often credited as the first person to circumnavigate Earth?

2. Isabella Bird, the renowned 19th century traveller, was the first female to be elected a Fellow of which august society?

3. What was the name of Shackleton's ship on the 1914 Imperial Trans-Antarctic Expedition?

4. Who accompanied Robert Peary to the North Pole in 1909?

5. 'Travelling – it leaves you speechless, then turns you into a storyteller.' Which 14th century explorer said this?

6. Where was explorer Sir Edmund Hillary from?

7. Which female British explorer, linguist and archaeologist was involved in the setting up of modern-day Iraq after the First World War?

8. Antarctic explorer Robert Falcon Scott sadly died on his final expedition, which was named after a ship. Name the vessel.

9. In 2018, Laura Bingham, Pip Stewart and Ness Knight were the first people to canoe the 1,014km length of a river in which country?

10. Can you name the titles of Levison Wood's 2015, 2016 and 2017 books, all beginning with *Walking*...?

11. Alexandra David-Neel was the first European woman to go where?

WORLD RECORDS

1. Nellie Bly was the first person to travel the entire world in less than 80 days, back in 1889. How long did it take her?

2. How old was Fred Distelhorst when he became the oldest man in the world to climb Mount Kilimanjaro?

3. When did Amelia Earhart fly across the Atlantic solo?

4. Who became the fastest person to visit all the EU member countries in the shortest amount of time?

5. In 2017, who set the world record for visiting every country in Europe in the fastest time – without flying?

6. Which TV show holds the record for being the longest-running travel series in history?

7. Climber Junko Tabei was the first woman to do what?

8. Which rock band became the first in history to play on all seven continents (including Antarctica) in 2013?

9. In 2019, who became the first documented black woman to visit every country in the world?

10. Which year holds the record as the 'safest year for air travel'?

11. How old was Lexie Alford when she became the youngest person in the world to travel to every sovereign country?

12. Adventurer Alice Morrison became the first woman to walk which Moroccan river?

RENOWNED WRITERS

1. In the 1930s, Robert Byron wrote *The Road to Oxiana*, oft-considered the first great travelogue. Where is/was Oxiana?

2. Elizabeth Gilbert's memoir *Eat Pray Love* took her to three life-changing destinations. What were they?

3. 'I come from Des Moines. Somebody had to' is the opening line to a book by which much-loved author?

4. *Full Tilt* was the first book by which Irish travel writer?

5. Which female author explored Antarctica in her book *Terra Incognita*?

6. In 1998, Pico Iyer released an eastern travelogue titled *Video Night in…* where?

7. The autobiographical novel *Papillon* by Henri Charrière famously focused on his incarceration on which island?

8. Sir Michael Palin's first travel tome was *Around The World in 80 Days*. But where did his 2019 'journal' take him?

9. Which USA hiking trail did Cheryl Strayed tackle in *Wild*?

10. John Steinbeck's *Travels with Charley* (his dog) involves a road trip around which country?

11. Which author released the part-fiction, part-travelogue 1987 book *The Songlines*?

12. What was the name of George Orwell's first novel?

COOL CRUISES

1. Which polar cruise company named a ship after the Antarctic explorer Roald Amundsen in 2019?

2. Starting in Puget Sound, USA, what would your final cruise destination along the Inside Passage be?

3. In which sea would you find the stunning Myeik Archipelago?

4. In which century did the Holland America Line launch?

5. If on an Arctic cruise, you sail to Franz Josef Land, which country are you in?

6. Koblenz, Rudesheim and Mannheim are usually stops on which European river cruise?

7. If you're stopping off at Siem Reap, Saigon and Phnom Penh which river are you cruising?

8. NEP and NWP are abbreviations for which cruising routes?

9. In which year did the beloved cruise ship *QE2* retire?

10. A Melanesian cruise would see you taking in Vanuatu, Papua New Guinea, the Solomon Islands and… which country?

11. Baja California and the Sea of Cortez are known for their grey and humpback whale-watching cruises. Which country would you be cruising?

12. New Zealand's five sub-Antarctic island groups make truly fascinating cruises. Can you name just one group?

SACRED PILGRIMAGES

1. What is the name of the annual Muslim pilgrimage to Mecca?

2. The Romeria El Rocio happens each year in which country?

3. It's called the Way of St James in English, but what is it better known as in Spanish?

4. In which Japanese region would you find the pilgrimage route known as the Kumano Kodo Trail?

5. The Via Francigena pilgrimage ends in Rome, but begins in which British city?

6. Bodh Gaya in Bihar, India, is an important pilgrimage site to the adherents of which religion?

7. In which country would you find the 2,243m-tall Adam's Peak, believed to be home of Buddha's 'sacred footprint'?

8. The North Wales Pilgrims Way finishes at which island?

9. On which continent would you find Mount Kailash Circuit, a pilgrimage to one of the world's most sacred mountains?

10. The pilgrimage to Señor de Huanca in Peru is undertaken by adherents of which type of Christianity?

11. The 65km-long Jesus Trail is a hiking pilgrimage beginning in which sacred city?

12. Which Northumberland pilgrimage site is only accessible when the tide is receding?

FAMOUS HIKES & TREKS

1. In which country would you tackle the W Trek?

2. Where can you walk the Overland and the Larapinta trails?

3. The hike to Everest Base Camp at the foot of the mountain is a nine-day feat. How high is Base Camp's altitude (in metres)?

4. Can you name New Zealand's popular Alpine Crossing, also the name of a UNESCO-listed national park?

5. Along which Mediterranean island's coast is the famous GR20 footpath?

6. The beautiful Chapada Diamantina is known for its trekking, including a wonderful day walk. Which country is it in?

7. You'll discover the colourful old mining town of Batopilas at the end of which Mexican walking route?

8. Waitukubuli National Trail is on which Caribbean island?

9. Papua New Guinea's rugged, rocky Kokoda Track is so dangerous, it must be hiked in which particular fashion?

10. The views of the Bhutanese Himalaya from the staggeringly high Chomolhari Trek are worth it, but where does the trail begin and end?

11. Canada's West Coast Trail was created to help shipwrecked passengers reach the shore in which year – 1907 or 1947?

12. In which country would you trek the famous Lycian Way?

TRAIN JOURNEYS

1. Salta, Argentina's Tren a las Nubes takes you somewhere out of this world. Where?

2. Which train (named after a colour) takes you from Pretoria to Cape Town in South Africa?

3. The Venice-Simplon Orient Express is one of the world's greatest luxury train journeys. But... where is Simplon?

4. On which eastern Caribbean island can you travel on a scenic railway on a 3-hour tour?

5. Fort William to Mallaig via the Glenfinnan Viaduct makes an appearance in which wizarding movie franchise?

6. The Bernina Express runs in one direction, from Chur in Switzerland to where in Italy?

7. What is the colloquial English name for the Shinkansen?

8. In which country can you journey on the Maharajas' Express?

9. Mexico's Chihuahua Pacifico railway is often known by the popular nickname for one of its trains. What is it?

10. Which railway passes through Wadi Rum in Jordan?

11. When riding from Kandy to Ella in Sri Lanka, in which village (close to Nuwara Eliya) would you stop on the way?

12. Amtrak's train that takes you from Louisiana to California, through Texas, New Mexico and Arizona is called what?

RAILWAY STATIONS

1. According to Guinness World Records, which train station has the most platforms of any station in the world?

2. Helsinki's Art Nouveau train station is flanked by several statues, called the *Men of the Future*. How many are there?

3. In which old city would you find Sirkeci Railway Station?

4. The stunning Maputo Central Station connects Mozambique to which three countries by rail?

5. London's Eurostar railway station is named after which saint?

6. In which city and country is the UNESCO-listed, Gothic-style Chhatrapati Shivaji Terminus?

7. São Bento Railway Station in Porto, Portugal, is known for its impressive display of what?

8. In which city and country will you find Atocha Station, known for its llight-filled, tropical garden?

9. Can you name the unusual red gate just outside of Kanazawa Station, Japan?

10. Malaysia's palatial, white Kuala Lumpur Railway Station embraces a mix of designs. When was it built – 1820 or 1910?

11. In which Australian city would you find Flinders Street Station?

12. In which London station did Harry Potter find Platform 9 3/4 (and tourists still search for it today)?

TRANS-SIBERIAN RAILWAY

1. In which Russian city does the official Trans-Siberian Railway begin: Moscow or Saint Petersburg?

2. The travel classic *The Great Railway Bazaar* was written by which author?

3. As well as the regular train services, a luxury "hotel on wheels" also operates on the routes. What is it called?

4. Perm is one of Russia's key Trans-Siberian stops. The city has a rather unusual flag, though, featuring which Arctic creature?

5. The route passes the world's deepest lake. What is it called?

6. The Russia-only Trans-Siberian route is one of the longest in the world. How many kilometres is it – 6,258, 7,725 or 9,258?

7. If not travelling to Mongolia or China, which Russian city marks the end of the Trans-Siberian route?

8. If you were to ride the Russia-only route without any extended stops, how many days would it take to ride?

9. On the Trans-Mongolian line, where do you change in Russia for Ulaanbaatar?

10. Does the Trans-Manchurian railway pass through Mongolia?

11. After which Russian stop does the Trans-Manchurian line change for China?

12. In which Chinese city does the Trans-Mongolian line end?

EXPLORING PATAGONIA

1. Which is bigger: Chilean Patagonia or Argentinian Patagonia?

2. How many national parks exist throughout Patagonia?

3. Can you name the iconic, granite peaks that define Torres del Paine National Park's landscape?

4. On which side of Patagonia would you find Lake Pehoé: Chilean or Argentinian?

5. UNESCO list three major glaciers to be found in Argentina's Los Glaciares National Park. What are they called?

6. The ancient handprints of Cueva de las Manos in Argentinian Patagonia date back approximately how many years – 5,000, 7,000 or 10,000 years?

7. Patagonia has two wild members of the camelid family (similar to llamas). Can you name one of them?

8. Who was Bernardo O'Higgins, the man whose name was given to a national park in Chilean Patagonia?

9. Cerro Chaltén is a very popular mountain on the border of Chile and Argentina. What is it better known as around the world?

10. Magellanic and Humboldt are two of the five what found here?

11. What species of secretive large cat is top of the food chain here?

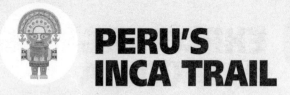

PERU'S INCA TRAIL

1. In which mountain range would you find the ancient citadel Machu Picchu nestled away?

2. In which century is it believed Machu Picchu was built?

3. Do you know when UNESCO first inscribed the Historic Sanctuary of Machu Picchu as a World Heritage Site?

4. How many days and nights does it typically take to trek the classic Inca Trail route?

5. What is the nearest town to Machu Picchu, often called the 'Gateway to Machu Picchu'?

6. From which two places can you depart via IncaRail or PeruRail to reach the Inca Trail or Aguas Calientes?

7. At the end of Runkurakay Pass, you'll come across Runkurakay's distinctive ruins. What shape are they?

8. The Inca archaeological site Phuyupatamarca earned which nickname, due to its high altitude?

9. Along the trail, you can hike to what was once the gate entrance to Machu Picchu. Can you name the gate?

10. Which leaf, beginning with "c", is chewed or turned into tea to help combat altitude sickness?

11. Which mountain towers over Machu Picchu?

12 Which river forms the Sacred Valley?

THE GALÁPAGOS ISLANDS

1. To which country do the Galápagos Islands belong?

2. Which influential 19th century scientist and naturalist is very much associated with the Galapagos, as it informed his famous theory?

3. Can you name the largest of the Galápagos Islands (by area)?

4. In which year was the Galápagos first declared a national park, and when did it become a UNESCO World Heritage Site?

5. Marine iguanas are a rare, unique species. But is it true that they are only found on the Galápagos Islands?

6. The sea lion-packed easternmost island in the Galápagos archipelago is also one of the oldest. What is its name?

7. Which 100-year-old giant tortoise was the last of his subspecies and sadly died in 2012?

8. The islands are known for their birdlife, too, including one creature with bright blue webbed feet. What is it called?

9. What's the name of the brightly-coloured crabs?

10. What is unique about where the endemic Galápagos penguin lives compared to other penguin species?

11. Of all the Galápagos Islands, only a few are inhabited by people. Can you name at least one?

12. Can you name the most populous town on the Galápagos?

ALONG THE SILK ROAD

1. During which century and Chinese dynasty was the Silk Road established, connecting the East and West for trade?

2. Constantinople, the capital of the Roman Empire, is now which modern city, and which country is it in?

3. In which Central Asian country would you find Almaty?

4. According to UNESCO, how old is the prominent Silk Road city of Bukhara, Uzbekistan?

5. In which city would you find Gur-e-Amir and the Registan?

6. In which central Asian country would you find the Silk Road city of Shahrisabz?

7. Lebanon's fourth biggest city, Tyre, was a Silk Road stop, though its nickname is connected to the sea. What is it?

8. The ancient city of Damascus was an important part of the Silk Road. In which country would you find it today?

9. Which Venetian merchant claimed (some dispute it) to have travelled the Silk Road in the 13th century?

10. The southern Silk Road route passed through a Chinese desert now nicknamed the 'Sea of Death'? What is it called?

11. Which Jiuquan landmark was a 'portal' for the Silk Road?

12. Which Chinese city, best known for the Bingmayong, marked the eastern end of the old Silk Road route?

ALONG THE NILE

1. The Nile has two key tributaries: the Blue Nile and another Nile named after a colour. Can you remember which colour?

2. In which country are the Blue Nile Falls?

3. Khartoum is where the Nile's two key tributaries meet. In which country would you find this city?

4. Can you name the traditional passenger boats beginning with "d" used on the River Nile?

5. Which southern Egyptian city is home to Elephantine, an island on the Nile?

6. In which large city on the Nile will you find Khan el-Khalili souk and the Mosque of Muhammad Ali?

7. Often a stop on Nile River cruises, what exactly is Beni Hasan?

8. Can you name the unusual double temple in Aswan, also a popular cruise stop?

9. The ancient monuments of Abu Simbel and Philae are protected by UNESCO. They were built by which people?

10. In which city will you find the incredible Karnak temple?

11. What is the name of the iconic 19th century hotel which overlooks the cataracts at Aswan, and whose former guests included Agatha Christie?

12. From Cairo, into which sea does the River Nile flow?

ALONG THE MEKONG

1. On which plateau does the Mekong River start?

2. Name the six countries the Mekong runs through.

3. Surprisingly, the Mekong is not among the top 10 longest rivers in the world. Where does it sit on the 'longest' list – 12th, 15th or 16th?

4. Which UNESCO World Heritage city in Laos is set on the confluence of the Mekong and Nam Khan rivers?

5. The cascading Khone Phapheng Falls on the Mekong are claimed to be the widest falls in the world. They are certainly one of the most beautiful natural wonders of which country?

6. What craftwork is the village of Long Dinh most famous for?

7. Krong Kampong Cham is a beautiful city along the Mekong, but in which country?

8. The 'Mekong stingray' is one of the world's largest what?

9. How many Thai-Lao Friendship Bridges are there (as of the year 2020) – 1, 2 or 4?

10. Which country's flag has a blue strip representing the Mekong River?

11. Each country has its own name for the Mekong. What's China's name for the river?

12. Which sea does the Mekong flow into?

GREAT WALL OF CHINA

1. In which region of China would you find the Great Wall: north, south, east or west?

2. Roughly how old is the Great Wall of China: is it over 1,000, 1,500 or 2,000 years old?

3. During which dynasty were the majority of walls still standing today built?

4. Is the Great Wall a third, half or two-thirds of the length of the equator?

5. What is the highest point (in metres) of The Great Wall?

6. Does the Great Wall reach all of these northern regions: Beijing, Tianjin, Gansu, Xinjiang and Henan?

7. Which part of the wall receives the most visitors each year?

8. The Dajiao Building is an oft-photographed spot at which part of the Great Wall?

9. To the west of Mutianyu is Jinshanling, which connects to which section of the Great Wall to the east?

10. A wilder section of the wall is called Jiankou. Do you know this name translates to in English?

11. Jiayuguan Pass and Shanhaiguan Pass are two of the three prominent passes along the Great Wall. What's the third?

12. With section of the Wall is sat beside a picturesque lake?

SENSATIONAL BORNEO

1. Borneo is Asia's largest island, but where does it rank size-wise with other world islands – second, third or fifth?

2. Which three countries share Borneo?

3. Borneo joins Java, Sumatra and Sulawesi as the fourth component of which incredible archipelago?

4. To the nearest thousand, what is the (2020) population of the endangered Bornean orangutan?

5. What is the name of the endemic monkey, known locally as the bekantan, known for its unusually long nose?

6. The *Rafflesia arnoldii* flower is found in Borneo's rainforest, but you'll smell it before you see it. What's its nickname?

7. Can you name just one of the colours adorning the feathers of Borneo's rainforest bird Whitehead's trogon?

8. What is Borneo's highest mountain?

9. In which Bornean state would you find the UNESCO-inscribed Taman Negara Gunung Kinabalu?

10. What is the name of the capital of Sarawak?

11. Which leopard species lives in Borneo's tropical rainforest?

12. Which national park is home to a 2,377m-high karst pillar, Sarawak Chamber, the world's largest cave chamber, and Deer Cave, famous for its huge number of bats?

OFF-THE-BEATEN-TRACK

1. Can you name all three of the Caribbean 'ABC' islands?

2. Liberia in West Africa is known for many things, including its beaches and its growing scene for which watersport?

3. In Saint Helena, you can visit the former house and empty tomb of which infamous French emperor?

4. Where would you find the otherworldly Fann Mountains?

5. Dili is the capital city of which lesser-visited Asian country?

6. Port Elizabeth and the Wild Coast make which South African cape an off-the-beaten-track gem?

7. In which country would you find the beautiful archaeological site of Butrint, a UNESCO World Heritage Site?

8. Chad's Zakouma National Park is notable for many wildlife species, not least for having the majority of the world's what?

9. Where in the Balkans will you find Bill Clinton Boulevard, and a shop named after Hillary Clinton?

10. Pohnpei has already popped up in this quiz book, but can you name the three remaining Federated States of Micronesia?

11. Paramaribo and Commewijne are two fascinating districts in which South American country?

12. North Cyprus has three castles built along the ridge of the Kyrenia mountains. Can you name just one?

UK
ISLANDS

1. Off which county's coast would you find the peculiarly-named Foulness Island?

2. Tresco, Saint Mary's and Bryher make up part of which British archipelago?

3. How many miles long and wide is the island of Lundy?

4. Off which Welsh county's coast would you find the puffin-packed Skomer Island?

5. In which century was Lindisfarne Castle, the jewel of Northumberland's Holy Island, built?

6. Papa Westray, Hoy and South Ronaldsay make up part of which popular Scottish archipelago?

7. A National Trust rope bridge links part of County Antrim mainland in Northern Ireland with which small island?

8. Which Scottish island is commonly known as 'The Queen of the Hebrides'?

9. On which UK island would you find Newborough Forest?

10. Jura in the Outer Hebrides is known for, among other things, its whirring whirlpool. What is the whirlpool called?

11. According to the National Trust, how many puffin pairs live on the Farne Islands – 3,000, 23,000 or 43,000?

12. Are the Channel Islands technically part of the UK?

TRICKY 50 STATES TRIVIA

1. Only one US state begins with the letter 'D'. Can you name it? Clue, its capital also begins with 'D'

2. Each of the 50 states has its own capital. Which state is Helena the capital of?

3. Which two regions are split into four states – North and South?

4. How many states begin with the letter 'M'?

5. Which of the 50 states is the biggest – by size?

6. How many states border their North American neighbour, Canada?

7. Meanwhile, only four US states border Mexico. Can you name them all?

8. Is Puerto Rico one of the USA's 50 states?

9. Each state has its own flag, but one state has gone rogue with a non-rectangular, red, white, and blue, swallowtail flag. Which state is it?

10. Every state has a two-letter abbreviation, for ease of writing. Which state is abbreviated as 'CO'?

11. Is the capital city of the United States, Washington D.C., technically one of the 50 states?

12. Which state was home to the FIRST official capital of the USA, once the constitution was ratified?

JUST FOR FUN

There's no rhyme or reason to this chapter (though you will find some road trip-friendly songs). These quizzes are designed purely for entertainment purposes.

We've got everything from the ultimate pub quiz round – which is perfect for an evening at home with travel-mad friends – to geeky trivia games to play on the road.

Identify quirky traditions, spot bizarre laws and solve puzzling airport codes, plus tackle an entire quiz where the only answers available are numbers, and a quiz full of place names you need to see to believe. Enjoy!

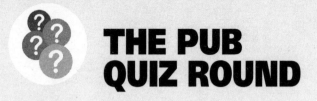

THE PUB QUIZ ROUND

1. What's the name of the largest of Niagara Falls' three falls?

2. Ireland has four counties beginning with 'C'. Can you name two?

3. Isabela and Fernandina are two islands belonging to which famous archipelago?

4. Which city has the distinction of being the 'world's southernmost capital'?

5. Featuring wrestling, horseracing and archery, in which country can you witness Naadam Festival in July?

6. What is the formal name for the world's greatest natural light display, the Northern Lights?

7. What is the official country name of Sri Lanka?

8. Tokyo is the current capital, but do you know the first capital city of Japan?

9. In which African country would you find the rock-hewn churches of Lalibela?

10. Do you know the three official languages of Belgium?

11. In which two Amazonian countries would you meet the indigenous Yanomami people?

12. St Michael's Mount is famously only accessible during low tide, but where in the UK would you find it?

UNUSUAL PLACE NAMES

1. Situated on the bend of a famous river, where would you find the small communal town of Toad Suck?

2. A Turkmenistan city shares its name with a biblical woman. What's the name?

3. Which of these is NOT a real place in Japan: Obama, Sega or Toyota?

4. Where would you find the idyllic island of Nosy Be?

5. The village of Made in the Netherlands sounds lovely, but what does 'made' mean in Dutch?

6. In 2012, three places with dreary names – Bland, Boring and Dull – decided to 'twin' together. True or false?

7. Where in the world would you find the small group of coral islands called Disappointment Islands?

8. The city of Uberlandia in Brazil was recently renamed after the car ride company Uber. True or false?

9. The hamlet of Shitterton has an unusual history, but which UK county can it be found in?

10. Is Australia home to the small town of Humpty Dumpty?

11. Does Canada have a city called Medicine Hat?

12. Finally, what's the story behind the name of the New Mexico town Truth or Consequences?

WORLD IDIOMS

1. In Polish, 'bulka z maslem' or 'it's a roll with butter' translates to which English idiom?

2. In Indonesia, *mencolek* has a specific meaning related to a common prank. What is it?

3. What does 'j'ai d'autres chats a fouetter' mean in French?

4. What does the phrase 'ter macaquinhos na cabecachuva' mean in Portuguese?

5. If a Brit says, 'you're getting on my goat', what are they telling you?

6. 'Gato con guantes no caza ratones' is a famous Spanish saying meaning what?

7. In Mandarin, what does 'playing an instrument to a cow' mean?

8. In English, you might say 'it's all Greek to me' when confused. Which place do the Czech substitute for Greece in that idiom?

9. If an American asks for 'your John Hancock', what is it?

10. Where might you say you 'belch smoke from the seven orifices from the head' when angry?

11. The Japanese idiom that translates to 'wear a cat on one's head' means the same as which English saying?

12. Where might you 'pager o pato' aka 'pay the duck' and take the blame for someone else's mistake?

LEGAL QUIRKS & MYTHS

1. In Quitman, Georgia, USA, which type of animal reportedly isn't allowed to cross the road?

2. An old law in which Italian city requires people (except funeral-goers) to smile?

3. What was it once illegal to forget when in Samoa?

4. During which set times can you legally buy alcohol in Thailand?

5. In Switzerland, a myth says you can't legally flush the toilet after which time?

6. What common beach activity can't you do on the beaches of Eraclea, Italy?

7. Where in Asia is chewing gum almost completely banned, with a potential fine of $100,000 USD?

8. Where in the Americas could you be fined for taking your feet off the pedals of your bike?

9. In Rio Claro, Brazil, which fruit are you forbidden to sell (and therefore can't eat)?

10. Talk about a plan ruiner! In which country is it against the law to fly with a rooster in a hot air balloon?

11. Why is it the law to keep your car clean in Russia?

12. Where could you possibly get arrested for 'holding a salmon suspiciously'?

CUSTOMS & TRADITIONS

1. The Easter bilby is which country's Easter bunny?

2. In which Latin American capital do residents roller-skate to their Christmas mass?

3. Is it customary to tip in Japan?

4. What is the tradition La Quema del Diablo in Guatemala, and when does it occur?

5. Why might you find young women being lightly whipped with a willow switch on Easter Monday in Slovakia?

6. Where might you play the drinking game 'pen-in-bottle'?

7. What happens during the Night of the Radishes in the city of Oaxaca, Mexico?

8. What happens during the USA and Canada's famous Groundhog Day tradition?

9. If you're travelling in Nicaragua and someone points toward something with their lips, what does it mean?

10. Which country has the old tradition of spitting on the bridge at a wedding?

11. If you're meeting a local in Venezuela, should you show up to the get together on time?

12. Clinking your beer glass in a bar is a big no-no in Hungary. Do you know why?

NATIONAL HOLIDAYS

1. What does King's Day celebrate, and in which European country does it take place?

2. St Patrick's Day celebrations in Ireland take place on which March date each year?

3. Hari Merdeka is the independence day of which Asian country?

4. France's Bastille Day is celebrated on which date each year?

5. Though it doesn't have the same date, Labor Day does fall at the same time each year in the USA. Do you know when?

6. On which day does Germany celebrate its Unity Day, commemorating the reunification of the country in 1990?

7. Dia de los Muertos, or Day of the Dead, is celebrated in Mexico on which exact date each year?

8. Where is Guanacaste Day celebrated, and what does it celebrate?

9. When do Canadians celebrate their national holiday, appropriate called Canada Day?

10. Where in the world is Waitangi Day celebrated, and why?

11. St George's Day is for the patron saint of which UK country: England, Scotland or Wales?

12. When does Independence Day take place in Chile?

NATIONAL ANTHEMS

1. The tune (not lyrics) of the UK's *God Save The Queen* is also used by which small European country?

2. *O Canada*, the Canadian national anthem, begins with which two lines?

3. Which European country has the world's longest anthem?

4. In which year did the *Star-Spangled Banner* officially become the USA's national anthem – 1901 or 1931?

5. Which African country has *L'Aube Nouvelle* as their anthem?

6. Which South-East Asian nation's anthem contains the lyrics: 'The path to glory is built by the bodies of our foes'?

7. In which year was South Africa's anthem adopted – 1991 or 1997?

8. And which five of South Africa's languages is it sung in?

9. *Lightning Over the Tatras* is the English translation of which European anthem's title?

10. Which country's national anthem's title translates to *Yes, We Love This Country*?

11. *Bilady, Bilady, Bilady* (My Country, My Country, My Country) is the anthem of which nation?

12. The words to *Kimigayo*, Japan's national anthem, are believed to be the world's what?

NATIONAL DRINKS

1. Which ingredients make up the classic Peruvian cocktail, the pisco sour?

2. What type of spirit is the classic Balkan *rakija*?

3. In which European country could you try Black Balsam?

4. Sake is the Japanese term for alcohol, but also refers to which specific type of beverage?

5. Which spirit should you use in the classic Cuban mojito?

6. Negroni and Aperol Spritz cocktails both originate from which European country?

7. In which country would you be able to try *boukha*, a distilled, fig-based drink?

8. South Korean *soju* is a clear alcoholic drink, usually consumed in which fashion?

9. Cognac is a distilled brandy named after a French commune, in which region of France?

10. What is *pulque*, and from which country does it originate?

11. Scotland is famous for whisky; which island, known as 'Queen of the Hebrides', is renowned for its distilleries and smoky peated whiskies?

12. Which country has a caipirinha (cachaça, lime and sugar) as its national cocktail?

WORLD CUISINES

1. Pico de gallo is a commonly-used salsa in which type of cuisine?

2. Often eaten by a gaucho and cooked by an asador, what is asado in Argentina?

3. Kimchi and bulgogi are two common types of food in which East Asian country?

4. What is the common name for traditional Japanese cuisine?

5. Cuy is often eaten in Peru. Do you know what it is?

6. Scandinavian *smørrebrød* is delicious and traditional. What is it made of?

7. *Rijsttafel* is a banquet of Indonesia dishes. But where would you most likely be eating it?

8. Cawl is the name of a soup made with meat and vegetables from which country?

9. Where does biryani, a mixed rice dish, originate from?

10. Where would you be most likely to try *pastéis de nata*, aka custard tarts?

11. *Sancocho* is a common Latin American meal. What type of dish is it?

12. In which African country would you have bunny chow, and what exactly is it?

NATIONAL DISHES

1. Italy has some world-famous dishes but it is often claimed that the national dish is Ragu alla ... what?

2. Ackee and saltfish, with onion, pepper and spices, is the national dish of which country?

3. Where in South America is ceviche – fresh raw fish cured in fresh citrus juice – the national dish?

4. A spicy fried rice dish, nasi goreng is the national dish of which country?

5. Traditionally prepared by men and often eaten with the right hand, what is Uzbekistan's national dish?

6. What is the national dish of Barbados?

7. Kabsa is the national dish of which country, and several others in the same region?

8. Uruguay's national dish is chivito, but what is it?

9. Which country has gallo pinto as its national dish?

10. Poland's hearty national stew is made with spicy Polish sausage and sauerkraut, but what is its name?

11. Bacalhau, which is dried and salted cod, is the national dish of which country?

12. Often described as 'the heart of Russian cuisine', what is pelmeni, the national dish of Russia?

AIRPORT TRIVIA

1. Do you know which airport sees the most passengers each year (including transfers)?

2. Can you name China's (and probably the world's) largest airport by size?

3. Where would you find the world's shortest commercial runway?

4. Several European countries have no international airport. Can you name one of them?

5. How many official airports are there in London, England?

6. In which year was the New York airport known as JFK named after President John F Kennedy?

7. Which civilian airport has the most runways?

8. Which Asian airport is regularly ranked as the best in the world by Skytrax and *Wanderlust* travel magazine?

9. What is special about Princess Juliana International Airport in Saint Maarten?

10. Can you name the northernmost airport travellers can actually use?

11. Which Scottish airport has a disappearing runway? Clue: it doesn't stay disappeared!

12. Which city is home to the John Lennon airport?

AIRPORT CODES

1. To which airport does code BHX correlate?

2. To which airport does code CHC correlate?

3. To which airport does code GIG correlate?

4. To which airport does code GOA correlate?

5. To which airport does code IAH correlate?

6. To which airport does code KIV correlate?

7. To which airport does code LGA correlate?

8. To which airport does code PEE correlate?

9. To which airport does code SEA correlate?

10. To which airport does code TAB correlate?

11. To which airport does code TAS correlate?

12. To which airport does code ZRH correlate?

ANSWER WITH A NUMBER

1. How high is Mount Kilimanjaro, the highest mountain in Africa (in metres) – 4,895 or 5,895m?

2. China has the largest number of neighbours in the world. How many countries share its border?

3. Greenland might be the world's largest island, but approximately how big is its population – 56,000 or 86,000?

4. Connecting the Atlantic Ocean with the Pacific Ocean, how long is the Panama Canal – 52km, 82km, 102km?

5. Dean's Blue Hole in the Bahamas is considered the world's deepest sinkhole. Just how deep is it – 160m, 182m or 202m?

6. Approximately how far are the Galapagos Islands from continental Ecuador – 500km, 750km or 1,000km?

7. Here's a tough one. How many time zones are there throughout Russia – 7, 11 or 13?

8. How many Baltic states (countries) are there in Europe?

9. London's Big Ben might remain silent for the near future, but typically it chimes at intervals of how many minutes?

10. How long is Peru's classic Inca Trail – 42km, 53km or 66km?

11. Roughly, how many islands does Fiji have – 222, 333 or 444?

12. Michael Palin famously dubbed it "The best travel magazine this side of Nanga Parbat", but when was *Wanderlust* born?

FROM A TO Z

1. How many countries begin with the letter 'A'?

2. Including England, how many countries begin with the letter 'E'?

3. Which of the 11 countries beginning with 'G' is the smallest (by population)?

4. One 'H' sovereign government is the jurisdiction of the Pope. What's it called?

5. The four biggest 'I' countries (by population) are India, Indonesia, Iran and...?

6. Which of the three countries beginning with 'J' is home to the Blue Mountain?

7. Oman stands alone as the only 'O' country. What continent is it on?

8. Only one country begins with the letter 'Q'. What is it called?

9. There are over 20 'S' countries around the world. How many begin with the word 'South'?

10. Can you name the smallest 'T' country, by population / area?

11. There are seven countries beginning with 'U'. How many of them begin with the word 'United'?

12. Yemen is the only country beginning with 'Y'. It's home to an island famous for its native dragon blood trees. Can you name the island?

GUESS THE COUNTRY

1. This country is landlocked by Romania and Ukraine.

2. In this city-state, you can stroll the neon, 101-hectare Gardens by the Bay.

3. Name the South Asian island nation home to the Ari Atoll.

4. You'd find Vianden Castle and Burgruine Brandenbourg in this petite country.

5. Here, you'd find the world's largest salt flat, plus Chile and Paraguay nearby.

6. The Devil's Pool forms this country's border with its neighbour, Zimbabwe.

7. A five-pointed star and white crescent moon adorn this country's dark green flag.

8. This Pacific country is a twitcher's dream. Its national bird the raggiana bird-of-paradise.

9. Chocolate Hills and the Banaue Rice Terraces are part of this country's landscape.

10. Name the nation that Bremen and the Black Forest belong to.

11. Legoland and the Little Mermaid sum up this country's best-known attractions.

12. This country is bordered by West Bengal, Meghalaya and Assam, among other Indian states.

TRUE OR FALSE?

1. Inhabited since at least 4000 BC; Skopje is the capital of Albania. True or false?

2. South Georgia and the South Sandwich Islands are a British Overseas Territory. True or false?

3. The city of Hull in England was once a UK City of Culture. True or false?

4. Peru shares a border with Venezuela. True or false?

5. Panama has two stars on its national flag. True or false?

6. The cities of Bishkek and Osh are in Kyrgyzstan. True or false?

7. The Republic of Madagascar is an island (not a peninsula). True or false?

8. The Federal Democratic Republic of Ethiopia is a landlocked country in East Africa and shares a border with Tanzania. True or false?

9. Japan has 13,000 islands in total. True or false?

10. There are eight countries with names ending in the suffix '-stan'. True or false?

11. Komodo dragons only live on Komodo Island in Indonesia. True or false?

12. Christmas Island exists (even if Santa doesn't live there!) and is technically part of Australia. True or false?

POPULAR TRAVEL TV

1. Who was Channel 4's original *Travel Man*, prior to Joe Lycett?

2. In which year did Sir Michael Palin's *Around The World in 80 Days* first air on BBC One?

3. In the first series of *The Americas* with Simon Reeve, which Americas do we visit: North, Central or South?

4. Can you name Hollywood star Ellen Page's LGBTQ+ travel docuseries for VICE?

5. The late Anthony Bourdain's CNN TV show for travel-loving foodies ran for 12 series. What was it called?

6. What were Joanna Lumley's start and end points in her series *Joanna Lumley's Hidden Caribbean*?

7. Which UK presenter's series' include *Britain's Best Walks*, *Walks with a View*, *Australia*, and *The Greek Islands*?

8. Can you name the brightly-clad long-standing presenter of the BBC's *Great British Railway Journeys*?

9. In which famous comedy series did Sir Michael Palin star before turning his attention to travel presenting?

10. Which award-winning chef stars in Netflix's foodie travelogue *Ugly Delicious*?

11. Karl Pilkington was the star of which comedic travel TV show?

12. Who narrated *Seven Worlds, One Planet*?

SONGS ABOUT PLACES

1. *Hotel California* is a song and album by which US rock band?

2. In Frank Sinatra's *Come Fly With Me*, which three destinations are name-checked?

3. Trance artist Infernal released a 2004 club smash, titled *From Paris to...* which European city?

4. *Istanbul* (not Constantinople) is a 1990 song by which band?

5. *Empire State of Mind* by Jay-Z and Alicia Keys refers to New York City as what kind of jungle?

6. Camila Caballo's heart is in which Latin American city?

7. Which famous city skyline do the Manic Street Preachers miss in their alternative 2013 hit?

8. The Proclaimers, it seems, were keen walkers. How many miles would they walk to get back to you?

9. *Budapest*, a song by a British male singer, isn't even really about Budapest. Who sang it?

10. The Clash's song *London Calling* is instantly recognisable, but in which year was it released – 1975, 1977 or 1979?

11. In *California Dreamin'* by The Mamas & The Papas, what colour are the leaves and the sky?

12. Which two African destinations are referenced in the lyrics of *Africa* by Toto?

CINEMATIC ADVENTURES

1. Which 'Way' does Martin Sheen walk in the film *The Way*?

2. Colin Farrell stars in a crime flick set in, and named after, which Belgian city?

3. Kenya is the true star of *Out of Africa* (1985), but with which two lead actors does she share the screen?

4. The epic *Fitzcarraldo* (1982) takes place in which river basin?

5. Where was the fabled island paradise in *The Beach* (2000) actually filmed?

6. *Walkabout* (1971) is a movie about children trying to survive which Australian region?

7. The film *Under the Tuscan Sun* sees a writer move to an Italian villa. Which Oscar-nominated actress plays the writer?

8. Which city do several retirees move to in the film *Best Exotic Marigold Hotel* (2011)?

9. *Lost In Translation* (2003) sees which two film stars befriending each other in a Tokyo hotel?

10. *Before Sunrise* (1995) is set in which romantic European city?

11. *Hunt For The Wilderpeople* (2016) is an adventure-comedy set in which part of the world?

12. *About Elly* (2009) looks at middle-class relationships in which Middle Eastern country?

MYTHICAL CREATURES

1. Scotland's national animal is which mythical creature?

2. Which mountain range does the yeti (abominable snowman) roam in Asian folklore?

3. The Druk thunder dragon is the national symbol of where?

4. Which mythical creature stands guard over Singapore's waterfront?

5. Huldufólk are elves in Icelandic folklore, but what does 'huldufólk' translate to in English?

6. Hungary's turul, also its national symbol, is a mythical type of… what animal?

7. Chollima or qianlima is a mythical winged horse. Which Asian capital has a statue of it?

8. Can you name the rock formation in Norway named after the mythic troll?

9. Lebanon and its capital, Beirut, has a deep connection with which famous mythical bird?

10. On which continent would a believer expect you to find Bigfoot in the forest?

11. In which century was the Loch Ness Monster first sighted?

12. Which mythical Chinese creature symbolises excellence, power, luck and nobility?

ANSWERS

AROUND THE GLOBE

P8. NORTHERN EUROPE

1. Lithuania
2. Stockholm
3. Finland
4. Denmark
5. Norway
6. Finland
7. Cape Nordkinn in Norway
8. Øresund Bridge, the 16km span that connects Copenhagen and Malmo
9. Estonia, Russia, Belarus and Lithuania
10. Sweden
11. Polar bear
12. Denmark
13. Lithuania
14. Freetown Christiania, created in 1971
15. 30,000
16. The 14th century (AD 1334)
17. Arctic Tern
18. Sweden's east coast and Finland's west coast
19. Latvia
20. Iceland
21. Norway
22. C) Ice cap
23. The Baltic Sea
24. Longyearbyen is a town in Spitsbergen, an island, which is part of the archipelago of Svalbard

P10. EASTERN EUROPE

1. Ukraine
2. Armenia
3. European Capital of Culture
4. 14th century
5. 38%
6. Ukraine
7. Walnuts
8. Ukraine
9. Georgia, Armenia and Azerbaijan
10. Romanian. Other minority languages include Gagauz
11. Romania (Palace of the Parliament)
12. Azerbaijan
13. Baku, Azerbaijan
14. Tbilisi, Georgia
15. Lviv
16. Armenia (it's the Areni-1 Winery)
17. 12th century
18. Belarus. It is open to the public for guided tours
19. Yerevan, Armenia
20. Moldova or Romania
21. Ukraine
22. Minsk, Belarus
23. Brasov and Râsnov
24. Georgia
25. Armenia
26. Shkhara

P12. CENTRAL EUROPE

1. Germany
2. Liechtenstein
3. Hundertwasser House
4. The Prague Astronomical Clock in the Czech Republic, built in 1410
5. Germany
6. Poland
7. Hungary
8. Poland
9. 130m
10. Plum
11. Würzburg and Füssen
12. Switzerland
13. Czech Republic
14. Gdańsk
15. All three!
16. Croatia and Italy
17. The Polish złoty
18. Salzburg
19. Pest
20. 1989
21. 25km
22. Paprika
23. Matterhorn
24. Bratislava, Slovakia
25. Prague
26. Liechtenstein

P14. SOUTHERN EUROPE

1. Spain
2. Vatican City
3. The Hellenic Republic
4. Eight
5. Andorra la Vella, Andorra
6. UK
7. Sicily
8. Brown bear
9. Sarajevo
10. Albania
11. Santorini
12. San Marino
13. Sofia, Bulgaria
14. Bosnia & Herzegovina
15. Tirana, Albania
16. Douro River
17. North Macedonia
18. Kosovo
19. Kotor gets its name from the Old Greek *katareo*, which means 'hot'
20. Pesto
21. Croatia
22. Serbia
23. Alentejo
24. Mdina
25. Bosnia & Herzegovina
26. Buñol, Valencia

P16. WESTERN EUROPE

1. France
2. Belgium, the Netherlands and Luxembourg
3. Belgium
4. Yes
5. Belgian chocolate
6. Slieve Donard, County Down
7. They are all Areas of Outstanding Natural Beauty (AONB)
8. Frog's legs
9. 2020
10. Bruges, Belgium
11. 54m
12. 19
13. Provence
14. *Bitterballen* are a thick meat stew which is rolled into balls. These are then coated in breadcrumbs and fried. They're a popular snack in the Netherlands

15. Yes, the UK has a bigger population.
16. South
17. The Grand Duchy of Luxembourg
18. Aberdeen
19. 17th century
20. Cliffs of Moher
21. Neoclassical
22. Old Quarters of Luxembourg City
23. Its dunes
24. Ben Nevis
25. Republic of Ireland
26. Approximately one third of the country

P18. RUSSIA

1. 10%
2. An administrative region
3. In Oymyakon, temperatures dipped as low as -67°C / -90°F back in 1993. It averages around -55°C/ -68°F
4. 3,530km
5. Red Square
6. Petrograd
7. Saint Petersburg
8. The Russian rouble
9. Saint Basil's Cathedral
10. Novosibirsk
11. Kaliningrad
12. Camomile
13. It is called Land of the Leopard
14. The Hermitage, Saint Petersburg, which is home to dozens of cats
15. Dumplings
16. The Caucasus
17. Saint Petersburg
18. Lake Baikal
19. Kazan
20. Empress Catherine the Great
21. Sakaiminato

22. White top, blue middle, red bottom
23. Kamchatka
24. The Siberian or Amur tiger
25. The Ural Mountains

P20. CENTRAL ASIA

1. Kazakhstan
2. Tajikistan
3. It's a Persian suffix for 'Land of'
4. Kyrgyzstan
5. Tajikistan
6. The collapsed gas crater is believed to have been burning since 1971
7. Kazakhstan
8. Samarkand
9. Kes kumay is essentially a grown-up game of kiss-chase, played on horseback
10. Tajikistan
11. Dushanbe, Tajikistan
12. Tashkent, Uzbekistan
13. Bukhara
14. Pulled noodles, meat and vegetables
15. Kyrgyzstan and Kazakhstan
16. Lake Iskanderkul
17. Kazakhstan
18. Yes
19. Tashkent Metro
20. The Asian elk
21. Picking up coins from the floor mid-gallop
22. The Asian golden eagle
23. Almaty, Kazakhstan
24. Turkmenistan

P22. MIDDLE EAST

1. Iran
2. The Cairo Tower
3. Oman
4. Turkey
5. The Church of the Holy Sepulchre is believed to be the site of Jesus's crucifixion
6. It is flipped upside down
7. Isfahan, Iran
8. 250m
9. Qatar
10. 9,000 BC
11. Petra, Jordan
12. Manama
13. Wadi Rum
14. Aqaba, Jordan
15. Doha
16. Luxor
17. Eastern European Standard Time (GMT+2)
18. Lebanon
19. Yemen
20. Istanbul
21. 82
22. Tel Aviv-Yafo
23. Jute plant
24. Hiking trails.
25. Beirut, Lebanon
26. Saudi Arabia

P24. AFRICA & INDIAN OCEAN

1. Morocco
2. 25,000
3. Livingstone
4. Fez
5. *Star Wars*
6. Sahara Desert
7. Ethiopia
8. East African Rift
9. Grande Comore (or Ngazidja in Swahili)
10. Arabic and French
11. Mint tea
12. A peninsula
13. Ethiopia
14. Zebra, wildebeest and gazelle
15. Mauritius
16. Malagasy
17. Rwanda
18. Blue, yellow, red, white and green
19. Injera bread
20. Zimbabwe
21. Dirham
22. Malawi
23. Kigali, Rwanda
24. Réunion
25. Mount Toubkal
26. Tanzania

P26. SOUTHERN & WESTERN AFRICA

1. South Africa
2. Senegal
3. Lesotho
4. The African penguin, sometimes called Cape penguin
5. Benin
6. The Gambia
7. Cassava and Plantain
8. Liberia
9. 10, plus some smaller islets
10. Freshwater hippos
11. Yes
12. Nigeria
13. Dune 45
14. Eswatini, formerly known as Swaziland (see Q 22)
15. Namibia
16. Sierra Leone
17. Palm wine

18. Eastern Cape and Western Cape
19. Zambia
20. Akodessewa Fetish Market
21. 300
22. Swaziland
23. Painted dogs or painted wolves
24. Fish River Canyon
25. Salt pans

P28. INDIA & SOUTH ASIA

1. Pakistan
2. The Maldives
3. Pokhara
4. India, Pakistan, Afghanistan and Tajikistan
5. Phobjikha Valley
6. Delhi, Jaipur and Agra
7. Eighth
8. Lahore
9. The Indian rupee
10. Nepal
11. Pakistan
12. The one-horned rhinoceros, also known as the Indian rhinoceros or the greater one-horned rhinoceros. The park is also known for a large number of tigers
13. Sri Lanka
14. Bhutan
15. Kathmandu, Nepal
16. Urdu and English
17. 30
18. Fuvahmulah Island
19. Wilpattu National Park
20. Hinduism
21. Bhutan
22. It means Royal Square. They are found in Kathmandu, Patan and Bhaktapur
23. Gujarat
24. Bengal tiger

25. West
26. Buddhism

P30. SOUTH-EAST ASIA

1. Yes
2. Bagan
3. Choose from: Bay Central Garden, Bay East Garden and Bay South Garden
4. Five: Myanmar, Vietnam, Singapore, Philippines and Timor-Leste
5. Petronas Twin Towers
6. Laos
7. Da Nang or Danang
8. Brunei
9. Ubud
10. Pho
11. East Timor
12. Cambodia
13. The Philippines
14. Denpasar
15. 30
16. Myanmar (Burma)
17. Saigon
18. Siem Reap
19. Choose from: Gili Air, Gili Trawangan and Gili Meno
20. Gliding mammals, sometimes called flying lemurs (though they are not lemurs)
21. Amazing street food! Hawker centres are the name of street food complexes and food courts in Singapore
22. Timor-Leste
23. Laos
24. Cebu
25. 30 years

P32. EAST ASIA

1. Mongolia
2. Busan
3. Kyoto
4. Chengdu
5. Gobi Desert, Mongolia and China
6. Pyongyang, North Korea
7. Altai Mountains
8. Shanghai, China
9. Cats
10. Snow leopards. China has the most
11. 101
12. Nara
13. 2,500
14. A yurt, which is a circular home that is usually portable
15. Pork bones
16. Honshu
17. South Korea
18. There are five 'a's in Ulaanbaatar
19. North Korea
20. Shinto Kanamara Matsuri
21. Portuguese egg tarts (*Pasteis de Nata*). It's not the only bakery to make them, but it has certainly become the most famous
22. Cherry blossom (sakura)
23. Taiwan
24. True! All of those things can indeed be purchased from select vending machines in Japan
25. Zhangjiajie Forest Park
26. The Star Ferry, founded in 1888 and still going strong

P34. AUSTRALIA & NEW ZEALAND

1. South Island
2. Australia with six, New Zealand has four
3. Aoraki Mount Cook
4. The Christmas Island crab. These giant red crabs live on land, and leave their burrows at the start of each monsoon to mate and spawn
5. The kakapo
6. Western Australia, South Australia, New South Wales
7. Hangi
8. Little penguin (*Eudyptula minor*), sometimes called the 'fairy' or 'blue' penguin
9. Yeast, or specifically, leftover brewer's yeast
10. South Australia
11. A fjord
12. Matamata on North Island
13. A platypus, sometimes called a duck-billed platypus
14. Maori and New Zealand Sign Language are the two other official languages
15. Auckland
16. Aurora Australis
17. Byron Bay
18. The Tasmanian devil
19. They are all Great Walks of New Zealand
20. Alice Springs
21. The quokka
22. Pohutu Geyser
23. False! Australia has more than 1.2 million feral camels
24. Abel Tasman was a Dutch explorer who became the first European to lay eyes on New Zealand

P36. PACIFIC COUNTRIES

1. Micronesia, Melanesia and Polynesia
2. Vanuatu
3. 40
4. Vanuatu. Tanna island is especially known for its cargo cults
5. France
6. False! The flag is blue with a yellow circle in the centre
7. Bikini Atoll is radioactive. A study suggests far more so than the Chernobyl Exclusion Zone and Fukushima in Japan, even 60 years after the USA tested weapons on the islands
8. Coconut cream
9. French Polynesia
10. Marshall Islands
11. Vanuatu. Men jump off wooden platforms with tree vines tied to their ankles
12. Bula
13. A drink made up of an extract of the piper methysticum plant. It is a herbal remedy but can have some interesting effects on the body, so read up before drinking!
14. Solomon Islands
15. Nan Madol
16. Nauru
17. Samoa
18. Nadi International Airport on Viti Levu
19. Papua New Guinea
20. Solomon Islands
21. Tonga is still a kingdom
22. Tuvalu
23. West Papua or Western New Guinea. It is part of Indonesia
24. Around 60
25. Tonga
26. Rugby

P38. UNITED STATES OF AMERICA

1. Arizona
2. 10
3. George Washington, Thomas Jefferson, Abraham Lincoln and Theodore Roosevelt
4. Florida
5. Yellowstone
6. Graceland
7. 184m
8. Utah
9. Northern Pacific humpback whale
10. Kansas
11. Vatican City and Monaco
12. Mackinac Island
13. Golden Gate Bridge may look a standard red, but its official colour is called 'International Orange', which is used in different industries to make sure it stands apart from other objects
14. Colorado
15. 1963
16. Monument Valley, Arizona
17. Maui
18. Cheese goes on to the base first, followed by any optional toppings, then the tomato sauce is put on top. Away into the oven it goes…
19. Yes, English
20. Massachusetts
21. Maine
22. Anchorage
23. Cascade Range

24. Horses
25. Bald eagle
26. Philadelphia, Pennsylvania

P40. CANADA

1. Canuck
2. True
3. True
4. Banff National Park
5. The plural of 'moose' is just moose
6. Prince Edward Island
7. Quebec City
8. Kebab
9. Poutine
10. Three, and the largest is Horseshoe Falls
11. Nunavut
12. False. Quebec and Montreal are French-speaking, while English is the dominant language in Edmonton
13. Beluga whale
14. Canadian Rockies
15. Churchill, Manitoba
16. Prisms
17. Alberta
18. Toronto
19. Three – the brown/grizzly bear, the black bear and the polar bear
20. Lake Louise
21. Brentwood Bay
22. Vancouver
23. The Rocky Mountaineer
24. Peninsula
25. Bay of Fundy
26. Yukon

P42. MEXICO & THE CARIBBEAN

1. Dominican Republic
2. Oaxaca
3. Dominica
4. Curaçao
5. Yucatán
6. Mexico
7. Southernmost
8. A leafy green vegetable dish
9. Puerto Rico
10. Cozumel
11. Grand Cayman
12. Grenada
13. Talavera tiles
14. Cenotes. Although they are found elsewhere, it is believed that the Yucatan has around 6,000
15. The United Kingdom
16. San Miguel del Allende
17. The Maya civilisation
18. Federation of Saint Christopher and Nevis
19. Blue agave
20. Copper Canyon – despite the name it is several canyons
21. Grenada
22. Pointe-a-Pitre
23. King Henri I

P44. CENTRAL AMERICA

1. Seven: El Salvador, Costa Rica, Belize, Guatemala, Honduras, Nicaragua and Panama
2. Guatemala
3. Keel-billed toucan
4. Guatemala, El Salvador and Nicaragua
5. True!
6. 30

7. Big Corn and Little Corn
8. Tico
9. The howler monkey
10. El Salvador
11. Honduras
12. Panama City
13. Belize
14. The north
15. Reptiles
16. Córdoba
17. Guatemala
18. El Salvador
19. Five
20. Chicken
21. Celaque National Park
22. Honduras
23. El Salvador
24. Volcán Tajumulco
25. Lake Nicaragua
26. Belize

P46. SOUTH AMERICA

1. Bogotá
2. Buenos Aires
3. True
4. Simón Bolívar. The currency is called bolívar and Venezuela's full name is the Bolivarian Republic of Venezuela.
5. Colombia
6. São Paulo
7. Salar de Uyuni
8. Atacama Desert
9. Aymara and Quechua
10. La Paz, Bolivia
11. Colombia
12. Capybara
13. Chimichurri
14. Portuguese
15. Guyana
16. Recoleta Cemetery, Buenos Aires
17. Paraguay

18. True
19. The name Copacabana!
20. Magellanic penguins
21. Suriname and Guyana
22. Aconcagua, Argentina
23. French Guiana
24. Peru
25. Pablo Neruda
26. Salvador

P48. THE ANTARCTIC & NEARBY ISLANDS

1. Ushuaia
2. Ross Ice Shelf
3. No, but it is a protected area
4. -89°C (exactly -89.4°C or -129°F)
5. South Shetland Islands
6. Choose from: crabeater, fur, leopard, Ross, southern elephant and Weddell
7. Port Lockroy
8. Emperor penguin
9. Lemaire Channel
10. USA
11. True
12. Yes
13. No
14. Horseshoe
15. Double
16. White
17. Lake Vostok
18. Trick question! None, and there are no permanent residents even today
19. Stanley
20. Three (2.8km)
21. Norway. The coast was named in the early 1800s, after the Crown Princess Märtha of Norway
22. True! All four of these species can be seen in Antarctica
23. Chinstrap penguins

24. It is a volcano and the southernmost active volcano on Earth
25. UK
26. False. Revenge is not a real island in South Sandwich, though Vindication is!

WHERE IN THE WORLD

P52. MATCH THE CONTINENTS

1. Africa
2. Europe
3. North America
4. Oceania (Australia)
5. South America
6. Antarctica
7. Asia

P54. MATCH THE COUNTRIES

1. Italy
2. Finland
3. Mongolia
4. Peru
5. Uruguay
6. Argentina
7. Namibia
8. Kazakhstan

P56. MATCH THE ISLANDS

1. Greenland
2. Borneo
3. Kangaroo Island
4. South Georgia
5. Isabela Island, Galapagos
6. Isle of Skye, Scotland
7. Palm Jumeirah, Dubai
8. Tavarua, Fiji

P58. MATCH THE US STATES

1. Maryland
2. Florida
3. California
4. Tennessee
5. Texas
6. Ohio

7. Alaska
8. Hawaii

P60. LARGE & SMALL COUNTRIES

1. Russia
2. Canada
3. China
4. Kazakhstan
5. Brazil
6. Peru
7. Algeria
8. Kazakhstan
9. Greenland. Part of the Kingdom of Denmark, it helps make Denmark the 12th biggest country in the world
10. Australia
11. China (based on official capital area only)
12. Democratic Republic of the Congo
13. Vatican City
14. Vatican City
15. Montenegro
16. The Seychelles
17. The Gambia
18. Saint Kitts and Nevis
19. El Salvador
20. Suriname
21. The Maldives
22. Nauru
23. 21 sq km
24. Federated States of Micronesia
25. Technically, Vatican City (once again)
26. Malta

P62. CO-ORDINATES & CLUES

1. The South Pole
2. The Giza Pyramids, Egypt
3. Mauna Kea, Hawaii
4. The North Pole
5. The giant pink rabbit atop Colletto Fava in Italy. (Seriously, get on Google Earth and search the co-ordinates now!)
6. Empire State Building, New York, USA
7. Quito, Ecuador
8. Volcano Island in the Philippines (Google Earth search the co-ordinates and zoom out!)
9. Madagascar
10. Greenwich Observatory in London, UK
11. Easter Island, Chile
12. Uluru/Ayer's Rock, Australia
13. Zaragoza, Spain
14. The Sacré-Cœur Basilica in Paris, France
15. Stonehenge, Wiltshire, UK
16. Alert in Nunavut, Canada
17. Invercargill, New Zealand
18. Lisbon, Portugal
19. The Atlantic Ocean, where the equator and Prime Meridian cross. It's a point in the ocean, and not an island, though weirdly it has been given the name of Null Island

P64. ON THE BORDER

1. Bolivia and Paraguay
2. Ecuador and Chile
3. No
4. Yes, it does, as well as Brazil and Bolivia
5. True. It also shares a border with Bolivia
6. 14
7. Choose from: Afghanistan, Pakistan, Tajikistan, Kyrgyzstan, Kazakhstan, India, Nepal, Mongolia, North Korea, Vietnam, Laos, Myanmar (Burma), Bhutan and Russia
8. No, it doesn't share a border with Azerbaijan (but it does with Tajikistan and Turkmenistan)
9. Choose from: Turkey, Russia, Armenia and Azerbaijan
10. No, quite the opposite! Sri Lanka is an island country
11. Choose from: Nepal, Sri Lanka, Bangladesh, Myanmar (Burma), Bhutan, China and Pakistan
12. Nepal, Bangladesh and China
13. Yes! Laos is bordered by Thailand, Vietnam, Cambodia, Myanmar (Burma) and China
14. 14
15. Choose from: China, Mongolia, North Korea, Kazakhstan, Georgia, Azerbaijan, Estonia, Finland, Latvia, Lithuania, Norway, Poland, Ukraine and Belarus
16. 17
17. Nine
18. Choose from: Austria, Czech Republic, Poland, Denmark, Switzerland, Luxembourg, France, Belgium and the Netherlands
19. Five
20. Choose from: Hungary, Montenegro, Serbia, Bosnia & Herzegovina and Slovenia
21. Finland, Sweden and Russia share borders with Norway
22. No, Denmark is connected to Sweden via a bridge
23. 17
24. Yes
25. Yes, it does, along with Uganda, Sudan and Somalia
26. False, they do indeed share a border (and attractions such as Victoria Falls)

P66. UNIQUE PASSPORTS

1. Fifth century BC (roughly the year 450BC)
2. Japan
3. Japanese passport holders can visit 191 countries without needing a visa
4. Singapore
5. Germany
6. Afghanistan
7. United Kingdom and United States are both tied, able to visit 185 countries visa-free
8. Red, green, blue, black
9. Navy blue
10. Yes, an outline of a kangaroo does appear on the front cover of an Australian passport
11. A moose!
12. Yes, along with designs of many Norwegian landscapes
13. Falcons. They have been introduced in an attempt to stop illegal smuggling
14. Red

15. False, though it does have the image of a crown
16. Gabon
17. Chrysanthemum
18. It features three moai statues
19. Crosses
20. Green
21. Old passports for UK citizens were red, from mid-2020 they are blue
22. True
23. New Zealand's passport is black with silver writing
24. Yes, it is true!
25. 31 states plus Mexico City

P68. AUTONOMOUS & DISPUTED STATES

1. Portugal
2. Tibet
3. Serbia
4. Nakhchivan
5. Tanzania
6. Island cluster
7. Russia
8. 1,600 kms
9. The Republic of China (as opposed to the People's Republic of China, which is the official name of the Chinese mainland)
10. Turkey
11. The Monastic Republic of Mount Athos
12. The Hong Kong dollar
13. Macau (often written as 'Macao')
14. Finland
15. Denmark
16. 2008
17. Inner Mongolia
18. Italy
19. Nuuk, Greenland
20. Azerbaijan
21. Corsica
22. Tiraspol

P70. UNINHABITED PLACES

1. New Zealand
2. Bouvet is the world's remotest island
3. 80%
4. Pigs!
5. Up to 50. In 2017, it was reported that 49 people called the island home
6. Whittier
7. Pacific
8. No, there are no cities in Antarctica
9. English
10. Volcano, or at least the remnants of one
11. Five - St Mary's, St Martin's, Tresco, Bryher and St Agnes
12. Snakes
13. Devon Island, Canada
14. Kikhpinych
15. California
16. Greece
17. St Kilda
18. It is around 1,600km from the coast of Africa (and 2,300km from Brazil)
19. No, according to the 2010 census, over 200,000 people still live there.
20. Marquesas Islands, French Polynesia
21. In 1995, the nearby volcano Soufrière Hills erupted and buried the town. The entire southern area of Montserrat remains an exclusion zone to this day

22. Auckland Islands
23. Calico
24. Route 66

P72. PEOPLE OF THE WORLD

1. Liverpool
2. 9 August
3. Around 100
4. Ethiopia
5. Loovuuz
6. Brazil
7. 16th century
8. 'Kiwi' is named after one of New Zealand's national symbols, the endemic Kiwi bird
9. 'People of the taboo'
10. Kenya and Tanzania
11. Gaulim
12. Men usually take their father's first name with the suffix son, while woman take their father's first name with suffix dóttir
13. The Ainu
14. Yellow
15. South-western
16. Guatemala, though some do live in Belize, El Salvador, Mexico and Honduras
17. Australia
18. South American cowboys
19. Pearls
20. An apprentice geisha
21. Reindeer
22. Haka
23. Suri women wear lip plugs or plates, often quite large
24. Belize

P74. CULTURAL & RELIGIOUS FESTIVALS

1. 5 May
2. Colour
3. Songkran
4. Chad and Niger
5. Papua New Guinea
6. Day of the Dead - 1st November
7. Wine!
8. Losar
9. 1966
10. Archery, horse racing and wrestling
11. Nassau
12. Inti, the Sun God
13. Five
14. Black Necked Crane Festival
15. Nagaland
16. The Grand Canal
17. Blood
18. Horses (and mules)
19. Pancake. It's often called 'Pancake Week'
20. Shetland. (Most notably, Up Helly Aa is celebrated in Lerwick, the Shetland's main town)
21. Gautama Buddha
22. Bolivia
23. Pingxi Lantern Festival
24. Harbin Ice Festival

P76. CAPITAL CITIES OF ASIA & THE PACIFIC

1. Kathmandu
2. Hanoi
3. Wellington
4. Phnom Penh
5. Tashkent
6. Seoul
7. Malé
8. Islamabad
9. Tajikistan
10. Vientiane
11. Port Moresby
12. Canberra
13. Naypyidaw
14. Kabul
15. Kazakhstan
16. Bishkek
17. Ashgabat
18. Beijing
19. Bangkok
20. Dhaka
21. New Delhi
22. Manila
23. Lebanon
24. Ankara
25. Bandar Seri Begawan
26. Thimphu

P78. CAPITAL CITIES OF AFRICA

1. Accra
2. Uganda
3. Lilongwe
4. Rabat
5. Pretoria, Cape Town and Bloemfontein
6. Madagascar
7. Lusaka
8. Eswatini (formerly Swaziland)
9. Victoria
10. Maseru
11. Kigali
12. Tunis
13. Freetown
14. Liberia
15. Nairobi
16. Harare
17. Dodoma
18. Botswana
19. Moroni
20. São Tomé
21. Chad
22. Port Louis
23. Praia
24. The Gambia
25. Addis Ababa
26. Kinshasa

P80. CAPITAL CITIES OF EUROPE

1. Tallinn
2. Athens
3. Tirana
4. Yerevan
5. Luxembourg (sometimes called Luxembourg City)
6. Bosnia and Herzegovina
7. Warsaw
8. Madrid
9. Sofia
10. Slovenia
11. Oslo
12. Lisbon
13. Chisinau
14. Bucharest
15. Georgia
16. Vaduz
17. Vienna
18. Kiev
19. Baku
20. Croatia
21. Minsk
22. Valletta
23. Dublin
24. Reykjavik
25. Andorra la Vella
26. Podgorica

P82. CAPITALS CITIES OF THE AMERICAS

1. Managua
2. Sucre
3. Quito
4. Brasilia
5. Venezuela
6. San Salvador
7. Ottawa
8. Port of Spain
9. Santo Domingo
10. Bogotá
11. Suriname
12. Georgetown
13. Lima
14. Washington D.C.
15. Haiti
16. Mexico City
17. Santiago
18. Buenos Aires
19. Kingston
20. Bridgetown
21. Paraguay
22. Roseau
23. Panama City
24. San José
25. Tegucigalpa
26. Montevideo

P84. MATCH THE FLAG OUTLINES

1. South Korea
2. Tunisia
3. Brazil
4. Albania
5. Lebanon
6. The Seychelles
7. Canada
8. Cambodia

P86. GENERAL UNESCO TRIVIA

1. United Nations Educational, Scientific and Cultural Organization
2. France (specifically in Paris)
3. 1,121
4. 53
5. Italy and China
6. They each have one UNESCO site
7. Two
8. 45
9. Bath
10. Aachen Cathedral
11. No, zero
12. True!
13. Dominica
14. It was removed due to the building of a bridge with four lanes through the cultural landscape
15. The Arabian Oryx Sanctuary of Oman
16. Singapore Botanic Gardens
17. 55
18. The Canary Islands
19. No, zero (surprisingly)
20. Three
21. The Galápagos Islands and the city of Quito
22. 75
23. 23
24. Yes, the Belize Barrier Reef Reserve System is classed as a UNESCO World Heritage Site. Surprisingly, none of Belize's incredible Mayan sites are UNESCO-listed
25. Yes, true! Ibiza is inscribed for its biodiversity and for its culture, including its archaeological sites and its fortified Upper Town
26. Morris Dancing is not on the list (yet)

P88. CULTURAL UNESCO WONDERS

1. 869 as of October 2020
2. France, of course
3. Lumbini was the birthplace of the Lord Buddha
4. Kyoto, Uji and Otsu
5. Bolivia
6. There are 10 octagonal temples
7. The Caribbean (northern) coast
8. Turkey
9. Robben Island
10. Wood
11. Thailand
12. Yes! It was inscribed 1984
13. Christianity
14. Antigua
15. Valletta
16. The Ifugao people
17. Rock paintings
18. San Agustín Archaeological Park
19. 2019
20. The Royal Botanic Gardens in Kew, London, the Singapore Botanic Gardens and the Botanical Gardens in Padua, Italy
21. A cat
22. Yes! It was inscribed in 2007
23. Saint Sophia's Cathedral
24. Oman

P90. NATURAL UNESCO GEMS

1. 213
2. Botswana, Southern Africa
3. Shark Bay, Western Australia
4. Peru
5. Limestone
6. Albania, Austria, Belgium,

Bulgaria, Croatia, Germany, Italy, Romania, Slovakia, Slovenia, Spain and Ukraine
7. Tubbataha Reefs Natural Park
8. India, stretching across six states
9. Uzbekistan, Kyrgyzstan and Kazakhstan
10. The Netherlands, Germany and Denmark
11. Tsingy is essentially the Malagasy term for 'where one cannot walk barefoot', which pretty accurately sums up those pointed towers
12. Jeju Island
13. Montenegro
14. Sinharaja Forest Reserve and the Central Highlands of Sri Lanka
15. Devon and Dorset
16. A crater
17. Spain
18. 400
19. A formerly large laurel forest, described by UNESCO as 'an outstanding relict of a previously widespread laurel forest type.'
20. Colombia
21. Vietnam
22. Mount Etna, Sicily, Italy
23. Guyana and Brazil
24. Slovenia and Italy

NATURAL WONDERS

P94. RARE RAINFORESTS

1. Tropical and temperate
2. The eight countries are Brazil, Peru, Colombia, Suriname, Guyana, Ecuador, Venezuela, Bolivia – plus the territory is French Guiana (a department of France)
3. The Congo Rainforest in equatorial Africa
4. Okapi
5. 12. There are two-toed sloths and three-toed sloths. Each sloth limb will have the same number of 'toes'
6. Costa Rica
7. Queensland
8. Malaysia, in Sabah, Borneo
9. South America
10. Tongass National Forest
11. Panama
12. Guyana

P95. BREATHTAKING FORESTS

1. Suriname in South America is just over 98% forest
2. Qatar, San Marino and Greenland
3. Taiga
4. Canada (British Columbia)
5. Forest bathing
6. Hampshire
7. Mangrove
8. Japan
9. Black Forest Gateau, a chocolate sponge cake with a rich cherry filling based on a dessert called Schwarzwälder Kirschtorte

10. Marten, sometimes known as nature's most adorable assassin
11. California
12. Gryfino in north-west Poland

P96. FLOWER POWER

1. Blue hydrangea
2. Ethiopia
3. Jacaranda
4. Provence
5. Washington D.C.
6. Medellín, Colombia
7. The lotus flower, which enjoys a sacred status and is a symbol of purity, beauty and fertility
8. Yes, it does
9. Thistle
10. Lisse
11. California poppies
12. Lupins

P97. WILD WETLANDS

1. The Pantanal
2. Botswana
3. Mokoro, a type of dugout canoe
4. Bolivia and Paraguay
5. Jaguar, the third largest cat in the world
6. The Camargue, located in southern France
7. A cowboy of the Pantanal
8. Kakadu National Park
9. Zambia
10. Romania
11. Keoladeo is a prime spot for migrating birds including Siberian cranes
12. The Ganges, Brahmaputra and Meghna rivers

P98. NATIONAL PARKS

1. Northeast Greenland National Park, Greenland
2. Asiatic lions. It is Asia's last home to these majestic animals in the wild
3. China
4. Chile
5. Tortuguero is Spanish for 'turtle catcher'
6. Its stunning 16 lakes linked together by waterfalls
7. Cairngorms National Park, Scotland
8. Yala National Park
9. Snæfellsjökull National Park
10. Australia: it is a mountain and National Park in Tasmania
11. France
12. India

P99. AFRICAN PARKS

1. Kruger National Park
2. Namibia
3. Masai Mara National Reserve and Serengeti National Park
4. Masai Mara National Reserve is in Kenya, and Serengeti National Park is in Tanzania
5. Elephant
6. Gabon
7. Agulhas National Park
8. Mountain gorillas
9. Virunga, DRC
10. Indri
11. The Ngorongoro Crater
12. Leopard

P100. USA PARKS

1. 62
2. Yellowstone National Park
3. Wrangell-St. Elias National Park & Preserve in Alaska
4. Arches, Bryce Canyon, Capitol Reef, Zion and Canyonlands
5. Yellowstone National Park
6. Tennessee and North Carolina
7. Yosemite National Park
8. The Joshua tree, which is commonly found in Joshua Tree National Park in California
9. Montana
10. Mount Cadillac
11. Denali National Park
12. New Mexico

P101. MIGHTY MOUNTAINS

1. Mount Kenya
2. Australia
3. Mount Everest
4. Chimborazo, Ecuador. It's just one degree from the equator, where the earth's bulge is greatest
5. Iran
6. Switzerland and Italy
7. 14
8. Honshu
9. Fishtail Mountain
10. South Africa
11. Nanga Parbat
12. Lotus Peak

P102. FAMOUS HILLS

1. Rome
2. Edinburgh, Scotland
3. The Chocolate Hills
4. A white horse
5. Derbyshire
6. One Tree Hill
7. Hill of Tara
8. The Earl of Durham's Monument, commonly called Penshaw Monument
9. Canada
10. Isle of Skye
11. Shimla
12. India

P103. FIERY VOLCANOES

1. Hawaii, USA
2. USA
3. The Ring of Fire
4. Ecuador
5. Costa Rica
6. Mount Teide
7. Campania
8. Indonesia
9. Popocatépetl is commonly nicknamed El Popo
10. Eyjafjallajökull
11. Caldera
12. Turkey

P104. DRY DESERTS

1. False. Approximately 20% of the world's deserts are sandy
2. Sahara Desert
3. Atacama Desert, Chile
4. Farafra, Egypt
5. Great Basin Desert
6. California, Utah, Nevada and Arizona
7. Wilfred Thesiger
8. Southern Africa
9. Mongolia and China
10. True
11. Bactrian, two humps
12. Almería, Spain

P105. HOT SPRINGS

1. Iceland
2. Frying Pan Lake in North Island, New Zealand
3. Dominica
4. Onsen
5. Budapest, Hungary
6. Up to 9m high
7. The Blue Lagoon
8. Yellowstone National Park
9. South Dakota
10. Denizli, Turkey
11. The city of Bath
12. Bali, Indonesia

P106. CURIOUS CAVES

1. Hang Son Doong, Vietnam
2. Mammoth Cave, USA
3. Matera
4. Cappadocia
5. Isle of Staffa
6. Glowworms
7. Slovenia
8. Cenotes are natural sinkholes, occurring when limestone bedrock collapses and exposes water beneath the ground
9. Scotland
10. Chile
11. Phraya Nakhon Cave
12. Belize

P107. OUT-OF-THIS-WORLD OCEANS

1. The Pacific Ocean is the largest and deepest
2. The Arctic Ocean is the smallest and shallowest
3. The Atlantic Ocean is considered the saltiest
4. Indian Ocean
5. Maritime Museum of the Atlantic in Halifax
6. The Mariana Trench
7. Pacific Ocean
8. Yes
9. Atlantic Ocean
10. Southern (Antarctic) Ocean
11. Around 70% of the world's surface is covered in ocean
12. Pacific, Indian and Atlantic

P108. INCREDIBLE ISLANDS

1. Greenland
2. Nauru
3. Cuba
4. Bouvet Island, a Norwegian overseas territory
5. 6,000
6. Ascension Island is part of the British Overseas Territory of Saint Helena, Ascension and Tristan da Cunha. Inaccessible Island is part of the Tristan da Cunha archipelago
7. Malta, Gozo and Comino
8. Socotra, Yemen
9. Rapa Nui
10. Indonesia
11. Rabbit Island is in Hiroshima prefecture, Japan
12. The Galápagos Islands, Ecuador

P109. SEAS OF THE WORLD

1. Caspian Sea
2. Indian Ocean
3. Caribbean Sea
4. Japan and Russia
5. Pacific
6. Adriatic Sea
7. Mediterranean Sea
8. Antarctica
9. Andaman Sea
10. China, South Korea and North Korea
11. Turkey
12. Mediterranean Sea

P110. PRETTY PENINSULAS

1. 'Paene' means almost, and 'insula' means island, making 'peninsula' an 'almost island'. Very fitting!
2. An isthmus is a narrow piece of land, connecting two pieces of land that are separated by water, whereas a peninsula is connected to just one piece of land, and is surrounded on three sides by water
3. The Arabian Peninsula
4. Kuwait, Bahrain, Oman, Qatar, Saudi Arabia, the United Arab Emirates, and Yemen
5. Dingle
6. Jutland
7. No, though the Alaska Peninsula extends around 800 km from the mainland
8. Gower Peninsula
9. Lizard Peninsula, Cornwall
10. South Australia
11. Costa Rica
12. Snæfellsnes Peninsula

P111. WONDERFUL WATERFALLS

1. Angel Falls, Venezuela
2. Atlantic Ocean
3. Guyana
4. Argentina and Brazil
5. Three
6. Walk behind it
7. Vietnam
8. Zambezi River
9. It is the widest waterfall in Europe
10. County Durham
11. Oahu
12. Ethiopia

P112. RAUCOUS RIVERS

1. The Nile, which is 6,650km long
2. The Amazon
3. Myanmar (Burma)
4. The Yangtze River, Asia
5. Iraq, Turkey and Syria
6. Scottish tennis star Andy Murray shares his surname with Australia's Murray River
7. 10
8. The Desaguadero River, Bolivia
9. The Nile
10. The Severn
11. The Whanganui River
12. False. Bahrain, Malta and Vatican City do not have rivers

P113. LOVELY LAKES

1. 16
2. Cumbria
3. Armenia
4. Wai-o-tapu
5. Salt
6. Lake Titicaca
7. Cambodia
8. Pink
9. Lakes Michigan, Erie, Ontario, Huron and Superior
10. Lake Victoria
11. Loch Morar
12. Guatemala

MANMADE MARVELS

P116. PERFECT PALACES

1. Lhasa, Tibet
2. According to the British Army, the Changing of the Guard takes place at 11am. This usually takes place on Mondays, Wednesdays, Fridays and Sundays, though this is dependent on weather and extenuating circumstances
3. Seoul, South Korea
4. The Winter Palace
5. The Habsburg dynasty
6. Sintra
7. Rajasthan
8. The Summer Palace
9. Amalienborg Palace in Copenhagen
10. There are 2,300 rooms in the Palace of Versailles
11. Florence, Italy
12. Interestingly, the Prince of Liechtenstein and his family officially reside in a palace that is also a castle, called Vaduz Castle

P117. DRAMATIC CASTLES

1. Bavaria, Germany
2. You'll find Leeds Castle in Kent, a few miles from Maidstone.
3. Windsor Castle, UK
4. Caerphilly Castle, a 13th century fortress not far from Cardiff
5. Slovakia
6. California
7. Aberdeenshire
8. Algeria
9. Takeda Castle in Asago, Hyōgo Prefecture
10. Bran Castle in Bran, near Brasov

11. Cartagena, Colombia
12. Namibia

P118. FASCINATING MUSEUMS

1. Grand Egyptian Museum (GEM), also known as the Giza Museum, Egypt
2. The Museo Nacional de Arqueología, Antropología e Historia del Perú (National Museum of the Archaeology, Anthropology and History of Peru) in Lima
3. Ukraine
4. Corones Museum, a museum dedicated to alpine history Unsurprising, given its location!
5. Croatia
6. The Terracotta Army. You'll find it at the Emperor Qinshihuang's Mausoleum Site Museum
7. True! All four of these museums exist in Japan
8. 19th century – it opened in 1881
9. Azerbaijan
10. Alkmaar
11. Sir Ernest Shackleton. Frank Wild, his right-hand man, is also burried there
12. Belgium

P119. ART GALLERIES

1. The Louvre
2. 1929
3. Van Gogh Museum, Amsterdam
4. Helen Martins
5. Museo de Arte Moderno, Mexico City
6. New York, Abu Dhabi, Bilbao and Venice
7. Girl with a Pearl Earring

8. Pergamon Museum, Berlin
9. Former prison
10. TeamLabs Japan
11. The Convent of Santa Maria delle Grazie in Milan, Italy
12. Cancún

P120. FAMOUS CITIES

1. León and Granada
2. Reutlingen, home to the 31cm-wide Spreuerhofstrasse, according to the Guinness Book of World Records
3. Smurfs! It's actually the third theme park in the world devoted to them
4. Manhattan, Brooklyn, Queens, the Bronx and Staten Island
5. People from Newcastle-upon-Tyne are referred to as 'Geordies'
6. Puerto Williams, Chile
7. Vltava River
8. Mdina
9. Nairobi comes from the Maasai phrase *enkare nyrobi*, which translates roughly to 'cool waters' or 'cold waters'. Give yourself a point for either!
10. Île-de-France
11. Yes, London, Windsor and Surrey are all UK places, and are also cities in Canada. Windsor and London are in Ontario, and Surrey is in British Columbia
12. Yokohama

P121. UNUSUAL TOWNS

1. Guatemala
2. Trullo; the plural is Trulli
3. 1947
4. Guyana and Suriname
5. Barnard Castle
6. Lake Thun and Lake Brienz
7. Guča
8. Blue
9. Mali
10. They are all examples of China's water towns, or canal towns
11. Dambulla
12. Rotorua

P122. EUROPEAN OLD TOWNS

1. Stockholm, Sweden
2. Warsaw
3. It dates back to the 13th century, making it around 800 years old
4. Tallinn, Estonia
5. Bryggen, in Bergen
6. Albaicín
7. Dubrovnik
8. *Les Miserables*
9. Salzburg
10. Carcassonne
11. The Grassmarket
12. Ronda; the old town sits on one side of the gorge, the new town on the other

P123. FAMOUS VILLAGES

1. Giethoorn is a car-free village, usually explored on foot or by bike
2. Hallstatt
3. Cornwall
4. Monterosso al Mare
5. Argentina
6. Malta
7. Bibury
8. Tunisia
9. South Africa; situated in the Amathole Mountains in the Eastern Cape province
10. Santorini
11. John O'Groats
12. It's a floating village (the residents fish for a living) in Halong Bay

P124. STATUES & MONUMENTS

1. The Statue of Unity, India
2. Aldeburgh, Suffolk
3. Underwater in the Mediterranean Sea, off the Italian Riviera coast
4. France
5. No, Buzludzha Monument is a socialist communist monument, erected in the 1970s
6. Senegal
7. Genghis Khan
8. 803
9. Kiev, Ukraine
10. Rapa Nui
11. Brussels
12. De Vaartkapoen shows a man emerging from a manhole cover, making a policeman trip over by tugging on his leg

P125. INCREDIBLE ARCHITECTURE

1. Shah Jahan
2. Barcelona, Spain
3. Just under 4 degrees, it was more until there were restorative and stabilisation works
4. Near Ouarzazate, in the High Atlas Mountains
5. Renaissance
6. William van Alen
7. His design was chosen in an international competition
8. Burj Khalifa in Dubai, United Arab Emirates
9. 26th century BC
10. Tel Aviv, Israel
11. Quebec City, Canada
12. The Eiffel Tower

P126. THE SEVEN WONDERS

1. 2007
2. Sadly, just one, the Great Pyramids of Giza
3. In the city of Alexandria, Egypt
4. The Temple of Artemis was a Greek temple in the ancient city of Ephesus. If it hadn't been destroyed, it would stand in modern day Turkey, in the Izmir province
5. Rio de Janeiro
6. Yucatán
7. The official number given by China's National Administration of Cultural Heritage is 21,196 km. And no, it can not be seen from space unaided
8. The Taj Mahal is a mausoleum complex
9. Concrete and soapstone
10. The Colosseum in Rome was originally called the Flavian Amphitheatre
11. El Castillo, also known as the Temple of Kukulcan
12. Siq which simply means 'gorge'

P127. ABANDONED PLACES

1. Centralia, Pennsylvania
2. Pripyat
3. Great Zimbabwe was a city in Zimbabwe, built between 11th and 15th centuries
4. Rubjerg Knude Lighthouse
5. Namib Desert
6. Villa Epecuén was flooded by water from Lake Epecuén, and disappeared over the course of several days. In 2009, the ruins began to remerge
7. South Georgia
8. From the 1930s onwards, mining for blue asbestos took place in Wittenoom, and the area remains a serious health hazard, despite attracting visitors (who are strongly advised against visiting)
9. Houtouwan
10. Matera, Basilicata
11. The Old Ghost Road
12. California

P128. ANCIENT CIVILISATIONS

1. Caracol is a Maya site
2. The Tairona people
3. The Federated States of Micronesia
4. 15th century
5. Athens, Greece
6. Nabatean
7. Guatemala
8. The Ancestral Puebloans
9. First century (AD 70)
10. Iran
11. Thailand
12. Carthage's archaeological sites are located in what is now the city of Tunis, Tunisia.

P129. FANTASTIC FOUNTAINS

1. Trevi Fountain, Rome, Italy
2. The Fountains of Bellagio
3. Swarovski
4. Midnight, or 00:00
5. Dubai, in the Dubai Mall. It is called The Divers' Fountain
6. Florida, where the Fountain of Youth Archaeological Park still exists
7. Singapore
8. Banpo Bridge, Seoul
9. Two
10. Geneva, Switzerland
11. Moscow, Russia
12. The Diana Fountain in Bushy Park, Richmond, is dedicated to the Roman Goddess Diana, while the Diana Memorial Fountain, located in central London's Hyde Park, is a memorial to the late Diana, Princess of Wales

P130. SACRED TEMPLES

1. Borobudur, Indonesia
2. Surya, the Sun God
3. 401 sq km
4. Kandy
5. Wat Rong Khun
6. Shwedagon pagoda, officially named Shwedagon Zedi Daw
7. Bhutan
8. 14th century
9. Jokhang Temple
10. Kyoto, Japan
11. India
12. Beijing, China

P131. MAGNIFICENT MOSQUES

1. Mecca, Saudi Arabia
2. Nur-Sultan, Kazakhstan (Hazrat Sultan Mosque)
3. Sultan Ahmed Mosque
4. Andalusia
5. Samarkand
6. Islam and Judaism
7. Four
8. The glittering white Grand Sheikh Mosque in Abu Dhabi
9. Casablanca
10. Ninth century
11. Three
12. Carpet and chandelier. Both have since been superseded by other mosques

P132. CHURCHES & CATHEDRALS

1. Ivan The Terrible, the First Tsar of Russia. His full name was Ivan Vasilyevich
2. Metropolitan Cathedral of Brasília, Brazil
3. Hallgrimskirkja
4. Colombia
5. Temppeliaukio is built into solid rock. It is sometimes called the 'Rock Church'
6. Salta Cathedral is a Roman Catholic cathedral
7. Novi Sad
8. 40,000
9. Its curved wall/roof of stained glass windows, which at certain times of the day or in sunlight shines rainbow colours throughout the entire church interior
10. No, the Sagrada Familia was unfinished at the time of architect Antoni Gaudí's death. It is widely believed that architect Jordi Fauli and team will have completed work by 2026
11. Westminster was once the site of an abbey until 1540. It is officially the Royal Peculiar, as opposed to a cathedral or a standard church. This just means that Westminster is subject only to the reigning monarch, as opposed to anyone else in the Church of England
12. Lebanon

P133 PEACEFUL MONASTERIES

1. Georgia
2. Petra
3. The River Wye, on the Welsh side
4. Meteora, in central Greece
5. A 'lavra' is a senior monastery, while 'pecherska' means 'of the caves'. It's also known as the Kiev Monastery of the Caves
6. Ostrog is a monastery for the Serbian Orthodox Church
7. You can choose from the Alcobaça Monastery, Batalha Monastery and the Monastery of the Hieronymites
8. Bhutan
9. Armenia
10. Austria
11. Skellig Michael
12. Bucovina

P134. BRIDGES & VIADUCTS

1. Brixby Creek
2. Prague, Czech Republic
3. Juscelino Kubitschek
4. Glenfinnan Viaduct
5. Q'eswachaka in Peru
6. Bosnia & Herzegovina
7. Hartland Covered Bridge in New Brunswick, Canada
8. The Bridge of Sighs. The rest are made up!
9. Uruguay
10. Isfahan, Iran
11. 134m
12. The neighbourhoods of Buda and Pest in Budapest, Hungary

P135. DAMS & RESERVOIRS

1. Six
2. Zambia and Zimbabwe
3. 220km
4. Akosombo Dam in Ghana
5. Nevada and Arizona
6. The Colorado River
7. Lake Nasser, Eqypt
8. Switzerland
9. Colombia
10. Gordon Dam is a curved arch shape, almost like a semicircle
11. British Columbia
12. Alqueva Lake, Alentejo, Portugal

GREAT JOURNEYS

P138. INTREPID EXPLORERS

1. Ferdinand Magellan
2. Royal Geographical Society
3. The *Endurance*
4. American explorer Matthew Henson, who Peary hired as an aide for the expedition due to his extensive experience at sea. (Their party was complete by four Inuit men, named Ootah, Seeglo, Egingwah, and Ooqueh.)
5. Ibn Battuta
6. New Zealand
7. Gertrude Bell
8. The *Terra Nova*
9. Essequibo River, Guyana
10. *The Nile, The Himalayas* and *The Americas*
11. Lhasa, Tibet in 1924. The country was out of bounds to foreigners at the time

P139. WORLD RECORDS

1. 72 days
2. 88 years old (and 180 days)
3. 1932
4. Sabin Stanescu, in 3 days, 22 hours and 39 minutes
5. Graham Hughes, for his record of 21 days
6. *Sereno Variabile*, an Italian TV show
7. Reach the summit of Mount Everest. She also became the first woman to ascend all of the Seven Summits
8. Metallica
9. Jessica Nabongo
10. 2017

11. 21 years old
12. Draa River

P140. RENOWNED WRITERS

1. Oxiana is a region in Afghanistan, on the northern border by the Aru Darya River.
2. Italy, India and Indonesia
3. Bill Bryson – it's the opening lines from *The Lost Continent*
4. Dervla Murphy
5. Sara Wheeler
6. Kathmandu
7. Devil's Island, French Guiana
8. North Korea
9. The Pacific Crest Trail
10. USA
11. Bruce Chatwin
12. *Burmese Days*

P141. COOL CRUISES

1. Hurtigruten
2. Alaska, USA (via British Columbia, Canada)
3. Andaman Sea
4. 19th century (1873)
5. Russia
6. The Rhine River
7. The Mekong
8. The Northeast Passage and Northwest Passage
9. 2008
10. Fiji
11. Mexico
12. The five island groups making up the sub-Antarctic islands are called Antipodes, Auckland, Bounty, Campbell and Snares

P142 SACRED PILGRIMAGES

1. Hajj
2. Spain – around a million pilgrims walk or ride to the little village of El Rocio each year at Pentecost
3. Camino de Santiago
4. Kansai
5. Canterbury
6. Buddhism
7. Sri Lanka
8. Bardsey, known as the 'island of 20,000 saints'
9. Asia
10. Catholic
11. Nazareth, Israel
12. The Holy Island of Lindisfarne

P143. FAMOUS HIKES & TREKS

1. Chile, specifically the Chilean Patagonia
2. Australia
3. 5,600m
4. Tongariro
5. Corsica
6. Brazil, located in Bahia state in the northeast of the country. The national park is known for its tabletop mountains, stunning caves and excellent walking
7. The Silver Trail
8. Dominica
9. The Kokoda Track must be walked in single-file
10. The town of Paro
11. 1907
12. Turkey

P144 TRAIN JOURNEYS

1. The clouds
2. The Blue Train
3. Simplon is a region in the Alps, naming the Simplon Pass. (There's also a Simplon in Switzerland.)
4. St Kitts
5. The Harry Potter series
6. Tirano
7. Bullet train
8. India
9. El Chepe
10. Hedjaz Railway
11. Nanu Oya
12. The Sunset Limited

P145. RAILWAY STATIONS

1. Grand Central Station, New York City, with 44 platforms
2. Four
3. Istanbul, Turkey
4. South Africa, Eswatini (formerly Swaziland) and Zimbabwe
5. Saint Pancras
6. Mumbai, India
7. Azulejo tiles – the traditional blue and white tiles of Portugal
8. Madrid, Spain
9. Tsuzumi Gate
10. 1910 – it's not as old as some people think
11. Melbourne
12. Kings Cross

P146. TRANS-SIBERIAN RAILWAY

1. Moscow
2. Paul Theroux
3. The Golden Eagle
4. Polar bear
5. Lake Baikal
6. 9,258km
7. Vladivostok
8. Seven days
9. Ulan Ude, Russia
10. No
11. Chita, Russia
12. Beijing

P147. EXPLORING PATAGONIA

1. Argentinian Patagonia
2. The Patagonia region contains 11 national parks as of 2020
3. Cuernos del Paine
4. Chilean
5. Upsala, Onelli and Perito Moreno
6. 10,000 years
7. Guanaco or vicuna
8. A former Chilean Head of State, who notably led Chile to victory against Spain in the Chilean War of Independence
9. Mount Fitzroy
10. Penguins – the five types are Gentoo, King, Rockhopper plus the Magellanic and Humboldt
11. The Patagonia Puma – it is believed there are around 50 as of 2020, and although shy there are an increasing number of specialist tours to track and see them

P148. PERU'S INCA TRAIL

1. The Cordillera de Vilcabamba mountain range, which is part of the Andes
2. 15th century (1450)
3. 1983
4. Most Inca Trail hikes take four days and three nights (though it is possible to have a shorter trek)
5. Aguas Calientes
6. The town of Ollantaytambo and the city of Cusco
7. Runkurakay is composed of a circular stone building
8. La Ciudad entre la Niebla, which translates to: 'The city in the mists'
9. Inti Punku, or Sun Gate
10. Coca leaf – the base ingredient for cocaine, it has been used by the indigenous people for thousands of years for its health benefits
11. Huayna Picchu
12. Urubamba

P149. THE GALÁPAGOS ISLANDS

1. Ecuador
2. Charles Darwin
3. Isabela
4. In 1959 it became a national park, and it was inscribed by UNESCO in 1978
5. Yes!
6. San Cristóbal
7. Lonesome George – he was the last known Pinta Island tortoise
8. Blue-footed boobies
9. Sally Lightfoot
10. The Galápagos penguin is the only species of penguin to live north of the equator
11. San Cristóbal, Santa Cruz, Isabela, Floreana and Baltra
12. Puerto Ayora in Santa Cruz

P150. ALONG THE SILK ROAD

1. Han dynasty in the second century BC
2. Istanbul, Turkey
3. Kazakhstan
4. Over 2,000 years old
5. Samarkand
6. Uzbekistan
7. Tyre is often called 'The Queen of the Seas'
8. Syria
9. Marco Polo
10. Taklamakan Desert
11. Yangguan Pass
12. Xi'an

P151. ALONG THE NILE

1. White Nile
2. Ethiopia
3. Sudan
4. Dahabiya (sometimes written as dahabeah)
5. Aswan
6. Cairo
7. An Egyptian cemetery
8. Kom Ombo
9. Nubian people
10. Luxor
11. The Old Cataract Hotel – currently known as the Hotel Sofitel Legend Old Cataract
12. Mediterranean Sea

P152. ALONG THE MEKONG

1. The Tibetan Plateau
2. They are Laos, Vietnam, Myanmar (Burma), Cambodia, Thailand and China
3. Twelfth
4. Luang Prabang
5. Laos
6. Mat-weaving
7. Cambodia
8. It's one of the world's largest freshwater fish and can grow even bigger than the Mekong catfish, which is renowned as another giant fish
9. Four, as of 2020
10. Laos
11. Lancang Jiang
12. South China Sea

P153. GREAT WALL OF CHINA

1. Northern China
2. Over 2,000 years old
3. During the Ming dynasty (1368 to 1644)
4. It is just over half (the equator's circumference is 40,075km).
5. Huanglouyuan, at 1,439m above sea level
6. Yes, plus 10 others!
7. Badaling
8. Mutianyu
9. Simitai
10. Arrow Nock
11. Juyong Pass
12. Huanghuacheng

P154. SENSATIONAL BORNEO

1. Borneo is the third largest island in the world
2. Malaysia (Sabah and Sarawak), Indonesia (Kalimantan) and Brunei
3. Greater Sunda Islands
4. 105,000 (104,700) according to the World Wildlife Organisation (WWF)
5. The Proboscis monkey
6. *Rafflesia arnoldii* is commonly called the corpse lily or the stinking corpse lily, due it its unpleasant scent
7. Orange, brown, a dark silvery grey (grey will do), dark blue, plus males have a bright red breast
8. Kinabalu, at 4,095m
9. Sabah
10. Kuching
11. The clouded leopard
12. Gunung Mulu National Park

P155. OFF-THE-BEATEN TRACK

1. Aruba, Bonaire and Curaçao
2. Surfing!
3. Napoleon Bonaparte
4. Tajikistan
5. Timor-Leste (sometimes called East Timor)
6. Eastern Cape
7. Albania
8. 60% of the world's Kordofan giraffes are said to live in Zakouma National Park
9. Pristina, Kosovo
10. Chuuk, Kosrae and Yap
11. Suriname

12. Saint Hilarion, Kantara and
Buffavento

P156. UK ISLANDS

1. Essex
2. The Isles of Scilly
3. Three miles long, and half a mile wide
4. Pembrokeshire
5. 16th century, in the year 1550
6. Orkney Islands
7. Carrick-a-Rede
8. The Isle of Islay
9. Anglesey
10. Corryvreckan
11. 43,000 pairs of puffins
12. No, they're not part of the UK. However, they are classed as a British dependency, and are located in the English channel

P157. TRICKY 50 STATES TRIVIA

1. Delaware
2. Montana
3. Carolina and Dakota
4. Eight – Montana, Michigan, Missouri, Maryland, Massachusetts, Mississippi, Minnesota and Maine
5. Alaska
6. 13
7. Texas, New Mexico, California and Arizona
8. No, but Puerto Rico is considered a territory of the USA
9. Ohio
10. Colorado
11. No, it's in Columbia, a stateless district
12. New York

JUST FOR FUN

P160. THE PUB QUIZ ROUND

1. Horseshoe Falls (also known as Canadian Falls), American Falls and Bridle Veil Falls
2. Carlow, Cavan, Clare and Cork
3. The Galápagos Islands
4. Wellington, New Zealand
5. Mongolia
6. Aurora Borealis
7. The Democratic Socialist Republic of Sri Lanka
8. Nara
9. Ethiopia
10. Dutch (Flemish), French and German
11. Brazil and Venezuela
12. Cornwall

P161. UNUSUAL PLACE NAMES

1. Arkansas, USA
2. Mary
3. Sega
4. Off the coast of Madagascar
5. Maggot
6. True! Bland is in New South Wales, Australia, while Boring is a town in Oregon and Dull is in Scotland
7. French Polynesia
8. False
9. Dorset
10. Nope, Humpty Dumpty doesn't exist, but it does have a town called Humpty Doo!
11. Yes, it's in Alberta
12. In 1950, it was named after a famous radio game show

P162. WORLD IDIOMS

1. 'It's a piece of cake'
2. *Mencolek* is the Indonesian word for tapping someone on the opposite shoulder, to make them look behind the wrong way. There isn't a comparable word in English
3. It literally translates to 'I have other cats to whip', similar to the English idiom 'I have bigger fish to fry', meaning you have something better to do
4. Literally, it means 'to have little monkeys inside your head', figuratively it means you have a crazy idea
5. You're annoying them!
6. It translates to 'a cat in gloves catches no mice', which means the same as 'nice guys finish last'
7. That whatever you were saying was falling on deaf ears, and not understood
8. In Czech, you'd say 'ke to pro me spanelska vesnice', which translates to 'it's all a Spanish village to me'
9. Your signature. It makes sense, given that John Hancock was the first to sign the USA's Declaration of Independence
10. China! This saying in Mandarin depicts the smoke coming out of your ears when enraged
11. 'A wolf in sheep's clothing'
12. Portugal

P163. LEGAL QUIRKS & MYTHS

1. Believe it or not, chickens!
2. Milan
3. Your wife's birthday
4. Between 11am to 2pm, and after 5pm until midnight
5. 10pm. We're not sure where this myth came from, but it's not a law exactly, though it might be expected if you live in an apartment building
6. You aren't allowed to build sandcastles
7. Singapore
8. Mexico, where both feet should be on the pedals at all times
9. Watermelon
10. New Zealand
11. So the police can easily read your license plate. Make sure you wash your rental
12. The UK

P164. CUSTOMS & TRADITIONS

1. Australia
2. Caracas, Venezuela
3. No, it isn't customary to tip in Japan. It can be perceived as rude, as good service is to be expected
4. Traditionally, on 7 December, Guatemalans set bonfires outside their house, 'burning the devil' the day before the procession of the Virgin of Immaculate Conception. Some cities will burn an actual model of the devil
5. This tradition is supposed to bring about beauty and good health
6. Sweden. The game is as it sounds: you tie a pen to some string, tie it around your waist, and drunkenly attempt to manoeuvre the pen into a bottle
7. On 23 December, locals will gather to carve oversized radishes and compete for a number of prizes. The tradition began in 1897
8. A groundhog (a large rodent) is pulled from the ground, and if it does not see a shadow, it's believed the groundhog has forecast an early spring. If it does see its shadow, it's thought that poor, wintry weather will continue for weeks to come. You can't make it up!
9. Exactly that. In Nicaragua, it is considered rude to point with your finger, so a head gesture and puckered lips in the direction they want to point is the natural response
10. This is an old Greek tradition
11. It's customary to show up a few minutes late, maybe 10 or so, to a meeting or get together in Venezuela, and indeed other parts of South America. Being early or bang on time can be seen as pushy, perhaps even greedy
12. While it's normal to 'cheers' with your eyes wide open with wine or another drink in Hungary, it's tradition not to clink with beer. Apparently, it dates back to the 1848 revolution. Austrians were seen clinking and saying 'cheers' and Hungary vowed not to do the same for 150 years

P165. NATIONAL HOLIDAYS

1. King's Day celebrates the monarch's official birthday in the Netherlands
2. 17 March
3. Malaysia
4. 14 July
5. The first Monday of September
6. 3 October
7. 2 November
8. Guanacaste Day is celebrated in Costa Rica on 25 July each year, to mark the annexation of the Nicoya peninsula in 1824
9. 1 July
10. New Zealand, to celebrate the creation of New Zealand and specifically signing of the Treaty of Waitangi in 1840
11. England
12. 18 September

P166. NATIONAL ANTHEMS

1. Liechtenstein
2. The lyric goes: 'O Canada! Our home and native land'
3. Greece, it has 158 stanzas
4. 1931
5. Benin
6. Vietnam
7. 1997
8. Xhosa, Zulu, Sesotho, Afrikaans and English
9. Slovakia. The title reads in Slovakian, Nad Tatrou Sa Blýska
10. Norway. The title reads in Norwegian, Ja, Vi Elsker Dette Landet
11. Egypt
12. The world's oldest words to a national anthem. They are from a poem written by an unnamed author in the Heian period (794-1185)

P.167 NATIONAL DRINKS

1. Pisco (a type of brandy), lemon juice, egg white and syrup
2. Rakija is a fruit brandy, with a high ABV percentage (40%)
3. Latvia, particularly in the capital, Riga
4. Sake is the common term for fermented rice wine, often drunk in Japan
5. White rum
6. Italy
7. Tunisia
8. Soju is typically served ice-cold, and poured neat into a traditional cup
9. Nouvelle-Aquitaine
10. Pulque is a thick, foamy, yeast-like drink made by fermenting the sap of an agave plant. It's often described as having a sour taste. It originates from Mexico, particularly central Mexico
11. Islay
12. Brazil

P168. WORLD CUISINES

1. Mexican
2. In short, it's how Argentinians barbecue. It's a specific technique of grilling meat, and the experience of a barbecue with friends
3. South Korea
4. Washoku
5. Cuy is the Peruvian name for guinea pig
6. Open sandwiches made of dark rye bread and a variety of toppings including cold cuts, fish, cheese
7. The Netherlands, in particular Amsterdam
8. Wales
9. India
10. Portugal
11. Sancocho is a broth, containing corn, meat, potatoes and a variety of other ingredients
12. South Africa. It's a hollowed-out loaf of bread, filled with curry

P169. NATIONAL DISHES

1. Ragu alla bolognese
2. Jamaica
3. Peru
4. Indonesia
5. Plov, aka rice pilaf
6. Cou-cou and flying fish. Cou-cou is made from corn meal and is similar to polenta
7. Saudi Arabia, and elsewhere in the Persian Gulf
8. Chivito is a big sandwich filled with thinly sliced beef steak (churrasco) topped with ingredients such as ham, tomato, melted cheese and fried or hard boiled eggs
9. Costa Rica
10. Bigos
11. Portugal
12. A type of dumpling, often with a variety of fillings

P170. AIRPORT TRIVIA

1. Hartsfield–Jackson Atlanta International Airport, Atlanta, USA
2. Beijing Daxing International Airport
3. Saba, a Caribbean island that is part of the Netherlands
4. Andorra, Monaco, San Marino, Vatican City and Liechtenstein do not have international airports of their own
5. Six, including Gatwick, Heathrow, Stansted, City Airport, Southend and Luton
6. 1963
7. Chicago O'Hare International Airport, Illinois, USA
8. Singapore Changi Airport
9. When a plane is landing, it flies right over a small beach, where visitors can get up close and personal with the plane
10. Svalbard Airport, Norway
11. Barra Airport, which lands on a sandy beach, and the runway disappears with the tide
12. Liverpool – its full name is the Liverpool John Lennon Airport

P171. AIRPORT CODES

1. Birmingham International Airport, United Kingdom
2. Christchurch International, New Zealand
3. Rio de Janeiro/Galeão International Airport, Rio de Janeiro, Brazil
4. Genoa Airport, Genoa, Italy
5. George Bush Intercontinental Airport in Houston, Texas, USA
6. Chisinau International Airport, Moldova
7. LaGuardia Airport, New York, USA
8. Perm International Airport, Russia
9. Seattle-Tacoma International Airport, Washington, USA
10. A.N.R. Robinson International Airport, Scarborough, Trinidad & Tobago
11. Islam Karimov Tashkent International Airport, Tashkent Uzbekistan
12. Zurich Airport, Switzerland

P172. ANSWER WITH A NUMBER

1. 5,895m
2. 14
3. 56,000
4. 82km
5. 202m
6. 1,000km
7. 11
8. Three
9. 15
10. 42km
11. 333
12. 1993

P173. FROM A TO Z

1. 11 – Argentina, Algeria, Afghanistan, Angola, Australia, Azerbaijan, Austria, Armenia, Albania, Antigua & Barbuda, Andorra
2. Nine – East Timor, Ecuador, Egypt, El Salvador, Equitorial Guinea, Eritrea, Estonia, Ethiopia and England
3. Grenada
4. Holy See
5. Italy
6. Jamaica ·
7. Asia
8. Qatar
9. Three – South Sudan, South Africa and South Korea
10. Tuvalu
11. Three – United Arab Emirates, United States of America and United Kingdom
12. Socotra

P174. GUESS THE COUNTRY

1. Moldova
2. Singapore
3. Maldives
4. Luxembourg
5. Bolivia
6. Zambia
7. Pakistan
8. Papua New Guinea
9. Philippines
10. Germany
11. Denmark
12. Bangladesh

P175. TRUE OR FALSE?

1. False, Skopje is the capital of North Macedonia
2. True
3. True, in 2017
4. False
5. True
6. True
7. True
8. False
9. False, Japan is believed to have 6,852 islands
10. False
11. False, Komodo dragons also live on nearby islands Rinca and Flores
12. True, Christmas Island is part of Australia

P176. POPULAR TRAVEL TV

1. Richard Ayoade
2. 1989
3. North America and Central America
4. *Gaycation*
5. *Anthony Bourdain: Parts*

Unknown. (*No Reservations* was his series for the Travel Channel and Discovery Channel)
6. Havana was her starting point, while Haiti was her end point
7. Julia Bradbury
8. Michael Portillo
9. *Monty Python*
10. David Chang
11. *An Idiot Abroad*
12. Sir David Attenborough

P177. SONGS ABOUT PLACES

1. Eagles
2. Mumbai (as Bombay), Peru and Acapulco Bay, Mexico
3. Berlin
4. They Might Be Giants
5. The lyric goes: 'Concrete jungle where dreams are made of'
6. Havana, Cuba
7. Tokyo
8. 500, and then 500 more if necessary
9. George Ezra
10. 1979
11. The lyric goes: 'All the leaves are brown, and the sky is grey'
12. Kilimanjaro (which rises like Olympus) and the Serengeti

P178. CINEMATIC ADVENTURES

1. The Way of St James also known as the Camino de Santiago, Spain
2. Bruges, in *In Bruges* (2008)
3. Robert Redford and Meryl Streep
4. The Amazon Basin
5. Ko Phi Phi Le, Thailand
6. The Outback

7. Diane Lane
8. Jaipur, India
9. Bill Murray and Scarlett Johansson
10. Vienna, Austria
11. New Zealand, specifically the forest and 'wilderness'
12. Iran

P179. MYTHICAL CREATURES

1. The unicorn
2. The Himalayas
3. Bhutan
4. Merlion – part lion, part fish
5. Huldufólk translates to 'hidden people'
6. A turul is a fictitious bird of prey, usually resembling a hawk or falcon
7. Pyongyang, North Korea
8. Trolltunga (literally, 'troll's tongue')
9. The phoenix
10. North America, in either the USA or Canada
11. 6th century (AD 565) – not that Nessie is a mythical creature of course!
12. The Chinese dragon

PICTURE QUIZ SECTION A
ANSWERS

P1. UNUSUAL ANIMALS

1. Axolotl, also known as the Mexican walking fish
2. Binturong. Known as the bearcat and found in South and South-East Asia
3. Aardwolf – found in Southern Africa
4. Collared pika
5. Red-shanked douc – only found in north and central Vietnam and Laos
6. Pangolin
7. Sunda colugo or flying lemur
8. Streaked tenrec
9. Coatimundi, often shortened to coati
10. Guanaco, found in South America and related to vicunas, llamas and alpacas
11. Tapir
12. Sloth

P4. ENDANGERED SPECIES

1. Sumatran rhinoceros – the smallest of the living rhino species and the only Asian one with two horns
2. Amur leopard – also known as the Siberian leopard
3. Silverback mountain gorilla
4. Bengal tiger
5. Bornean orangutan
6. Black-and-white ruffed lemur
7. Giant river otter, which can grow up to 1.7 metres long
8. Leatherback sea turtle

P6. AFRICAN ANIMALS

1. Cape buffalo
2. African elephant
3. African wild dog
4. Cheetah
5. Lion
6. Wildebeest
7. Mandrill
8. Gemsbok (oryx gazella)

P8. UNUSUAL CATS

1. Caracal
2. Sand cat
3. Ocelot
4. Jaguarundi
5. Margay
6. Flat-headed cat
7. Oncilla also known as a Tigrillo
8. Pallas's cat

P10. BEARS OF THE WORLD

1. Andean (spectacled) bear
2. Polar bear
3. American black bear
4. Brown bear
5. Giant panda
6. Sun bear
7. Asiatic black bear
8. Sloth bear

P12. RARE BIRDS

1. Red-crowned crane
2. Great Indian bustard
3. Kakapo
4. Galapagos penguin
5. California condor
6. Bald eagle
7. Blue-throated macaw
8. Black-tailed godwit

P14. COLOURFUL BIRDS

1. Andean cock-of-the-rock (Give yourself a point for just 'cock-of-the-rock')
2. Scarlet macaw
3. Greater bird-of-paradise (Give yourself a point for just 'bird-of-paradise')
4. Turquoise-browed motmot
5. Keel-billed toucan (Give yourself a point for just 'toucan')
6. Lilac-breasted roller
7. Lady Gouldian finch
8. Resplendent quetzal (Give yourself a point for just 'quetzal')

P16. FAMOUS ANIMALS

1. Jonathan the tortoise, Saint Helena, who is the oldest known living terrestrial animal in the world. It's believed he was hatched in 1832
2. Roger the kangaroo, who shot to fame for his muscular physique
3. Fungie the Dingle dolphin is a friendly bottlenosed dolphin who's been a popular sight off Ireland's Dingle Peninsula since 1983
4. Punxsutawney Phil, the groundhog the USA unveils each Groundhog Day

PICTURE QUIZ SECTION B

ANSWERS

P1. ANCIENT SITES

1. Petra, Jordan (Specifically the treasury, Al-Khazneh)
2. Sphinx, Egypt
3. Tikal, Guatemala (Specifically the Temple of the Great Jaguar)
4. Kuelap, Peru
5. Caracol, Belize
6. Chichén Itzá, Mexico (Specifically El Castillo, the Kukulkan Temple)
7. Pompeii, Italy
8. The Imperial City of Hue, Vietnam
9. Machu Picchu, Peru
10. Nan Madol, Federated States of Micronesia (Specifically the town walls)
11. Ciudad Perdida, Colombia
12. Angkor Wat, Cambodia

P4. GUESS THE UNESCO SITE

1. Perito Moreno Glacier in Los Glaciares National Park, Argentina
2. The city of Potosi, Bolivia
3. Stonehenge, England
4. Park Güell, Barcelona, Spain
5. Borobudur Temple, Indonesia
6. Meteora, Greece
7. Lalibela, Ethiopia
8. Prague, Czech Republic

P6. WHERE WAS THIS TAKEN

1. Galápagos Islands
2. Luang Prabang, Laos
3. Masai Mara National Reserve, Kenya
4. Kinderdijk, the Netherlands
5. Kyoto, Japan
6. Torres del Paine National Park, Chile
7. Neist Point, Isle of Skye, Scotland
8. Stockholm, Sweden

P8. MATCH THE STREET SIGNS

1. Austria
2. Japan
3. Russia
4. England
5. Colombia
6. New Zealand
7. France
8. Spain

P10. UNUSUAL STATUES

1. Colombia
2. Norway
3. India
4. Ukraine
5. Easter Island, Chile
6. Czech Republic
7. Kyrgyzstan
8. USA

P12. COLOURFUL BUILDINGS

1. Italy (Cinque Terre)
2. Greenland (Nuuk)
3. Singapore (Little India)
4. Italy (Burano, Venice)
5. Argentina (La Boca, Buenos Aires)
6. South Africa (Bo Kaap, Cape Town)
7. Indonesia (Java)
8. Cuba (Havana)

P14. UNUSUAL FLAGS

1. Kyrgyzstan
2. Dominica
3. Bhutan
4. Serbia
5. Denmark
6. San Marino
7. Azerbaijan
8. Tanzania
9. Thailand
10. Zimbabwe
11. Portugal
12. Papua New Guinea

CREDITS & SOURCES

SITES FREQUENTLY REFERENCED:

countries-ofthe-world.com/largest-countries.html

countries-ofthe-world.com/smallest-countries.html

henleypassportindex.com

worldpopulationreview.com/

nasa.gov/

guinnessworldrecords.com/

UNESCO whc.unesco.org

world-airport-codes.com/

worldwildlife.org/

airportcod.es/#

nationalgeographic.co.uk

http://towerofpisa.org/leaning-tower-of-pisa-facts/

South Africa National Parks sanparks.org/

Tourism Australia australia.com/en-us

US National Parks Service nps.gov/index.htm

Guggenheim guggenheim.org/

Van Gogh vangoghmuseum.nl/

Visit Europe visiteurope.com/en

sedlecossuary.com/

history.co.uk/

hallgrimskirkja.is/um-hallgrimskirkju/

winchester-cathedral.org.uk/

edition.cnn.com/travel/article/sheikh-zayed-grand-mosque-abu-dhabi/index.html

sumela.com/

China's National Administration of Cultural Heritage

sydney.com/

tripsavvy.com/everything-you-need-to-know-about-lake-kariba-4138385

lonelyplanet.com/montenegro/coastal-montenegro/kotor/attractions/kotor-city-walls/a/poi-sig/1265447/360156

opodo.co.uk/

landmarktrust.org.uk/lundyisland/day-trips/

nationaltrust.org.uk

hurtigruten.co.uk/our-ships/

visitislesofscilly.com/

ascension.gov.ac/lifestyle-and-employment/living-here-2

businessinsider.com/best-passports-most-countries-no-visa-henley-index-2020-1?r=US&IR=T

livelearn.ca/article/about-canada/did-you-know-that-80-per-cent-of-canada-is-uninhabited-learn-more-about-canadas-geography/

immigration.gov.pn/community/the_people/index.html

melbourne.vic.gov.au/about-melbourne/melbourne-profile/Pages/facts-about-melbourne.aspx

natureconservancy.ca/en/what-we-do/resource-centre/featured-species/mammals/grizzly_bear.html

Note: This list is not exhaustive but is a representative sample of sites used when fact-checking.